ASTRA ZERO

RETRO
SINNERS

A SOMEWHAT EROTIC MISMATCHED
COLLECTION OF RETRO INSPIRED
ARTWORK CENTRED AROUND THE
MALE BODY WITH A DARK, HUMOROUS
AND SOMETIMES HORROR INSPIRED
TWIST

astrazero.com  @astrazero

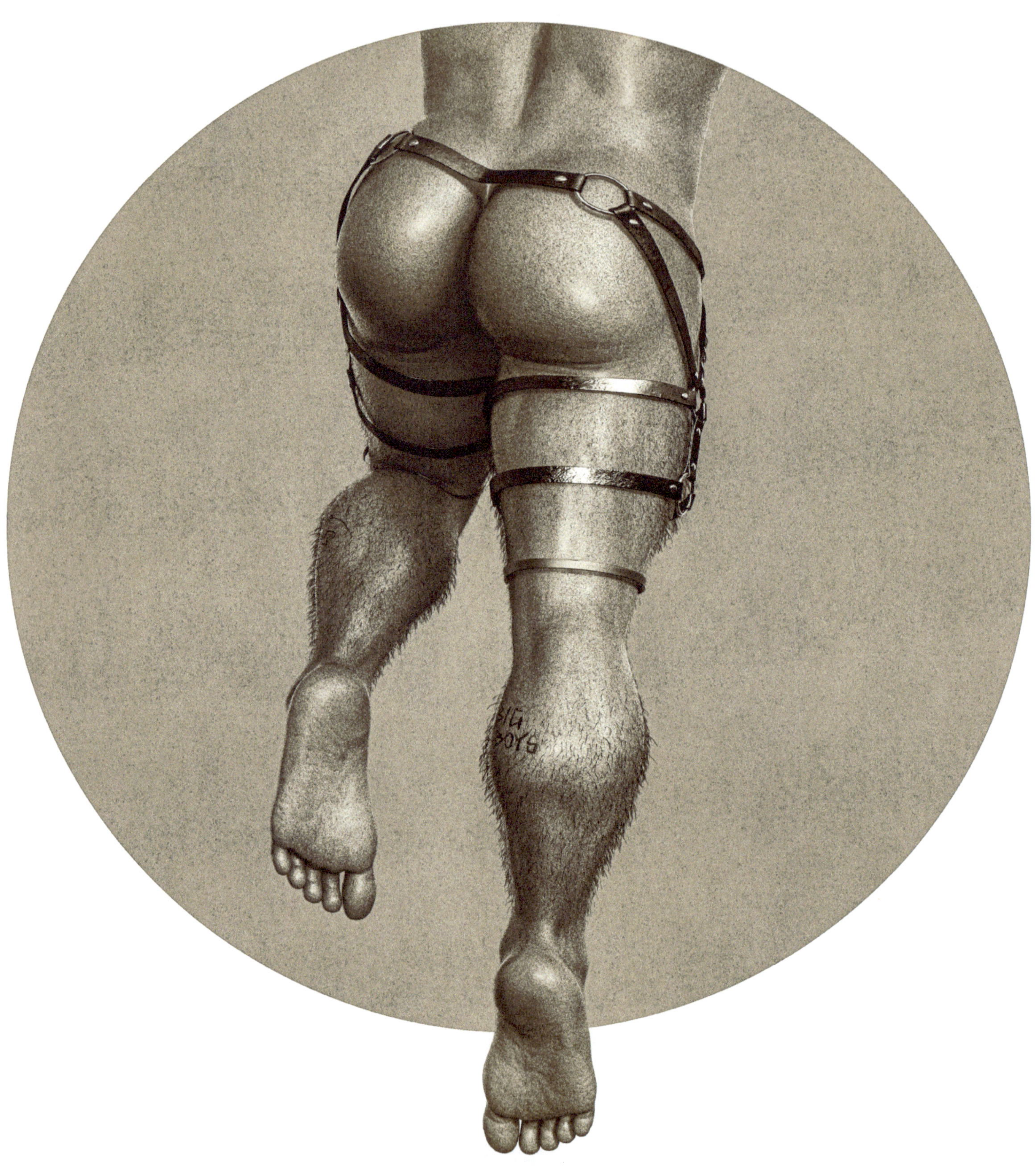

BIG
BOYS

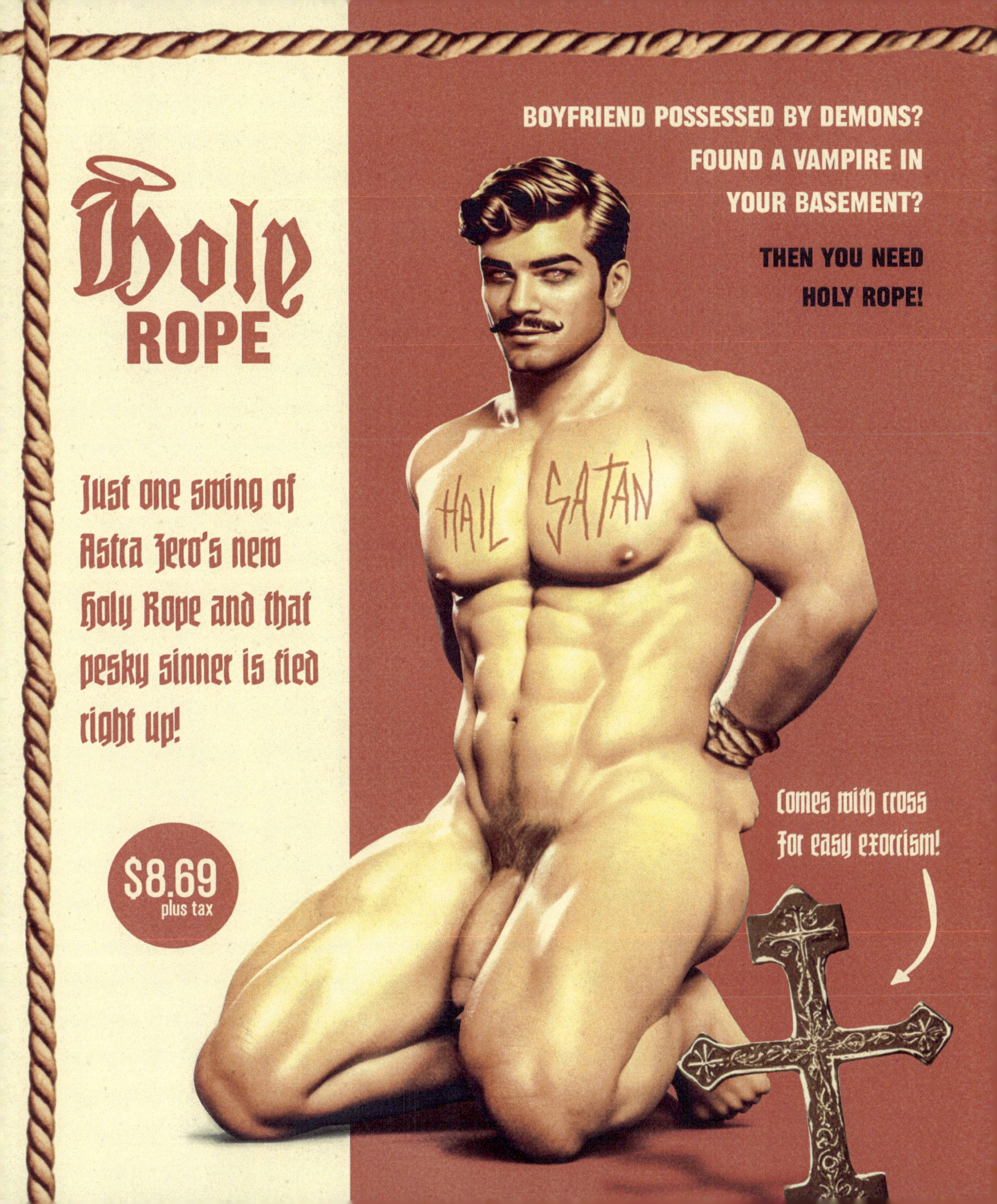

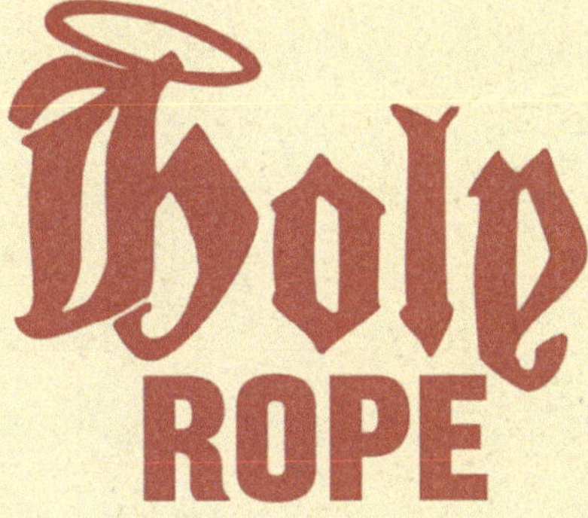

Holy ROPE

Just one swing of Astra Zero's new Holy Rope and that pesky sinner is tied right up!

$8.69
plus tax

BOYFRIEND POSSESSED BY DEMONS? FOUND A VAMPIRE IN YOUR BASEMENT?

THEN YOU NEED HOLY ROPE!

Comes with cross for easy exorcism!

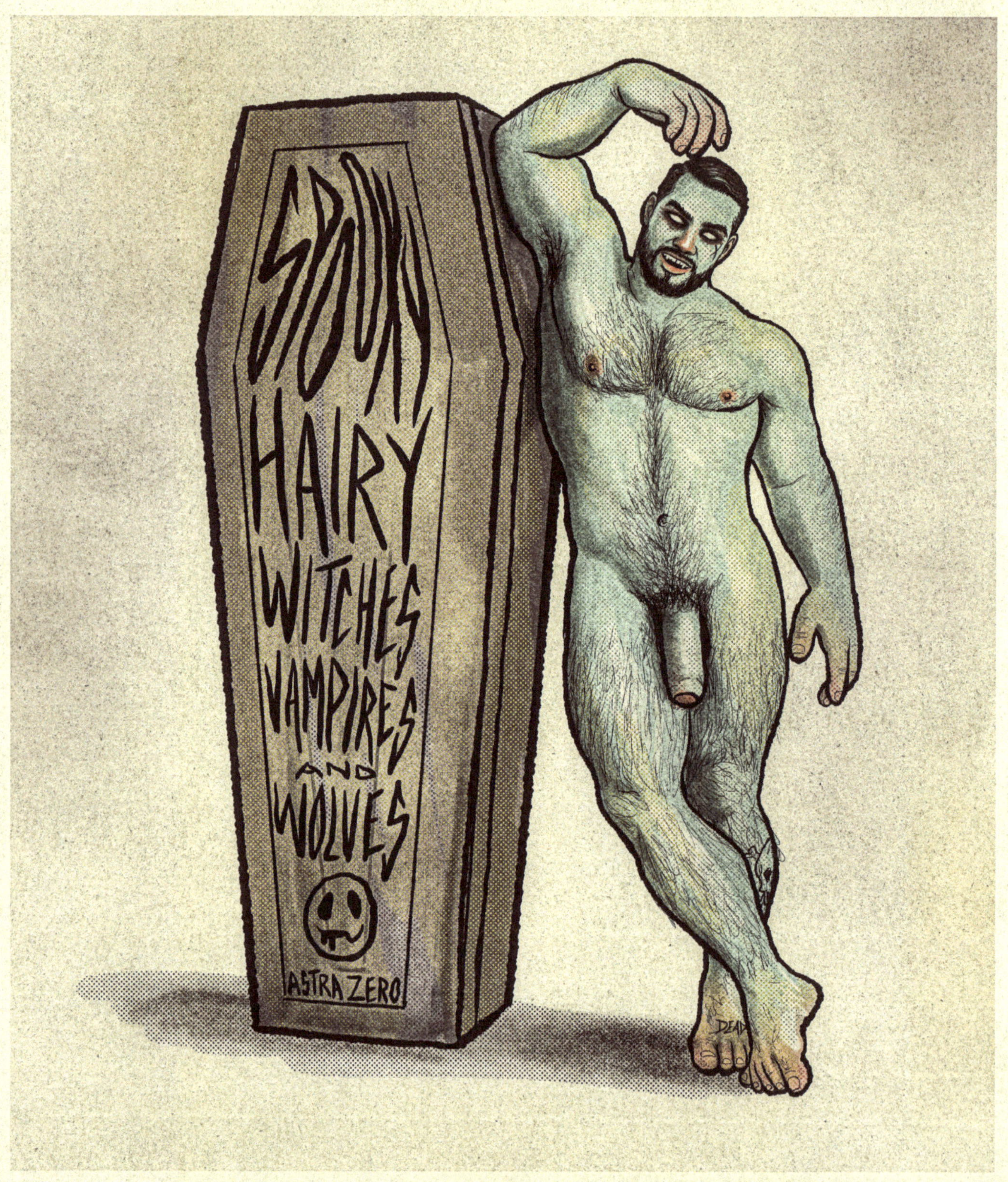

SPOOKY
HAIRY
WITCHES
VAMPIRES
AND
WOLVES
IASTRA ZERO
DEAD

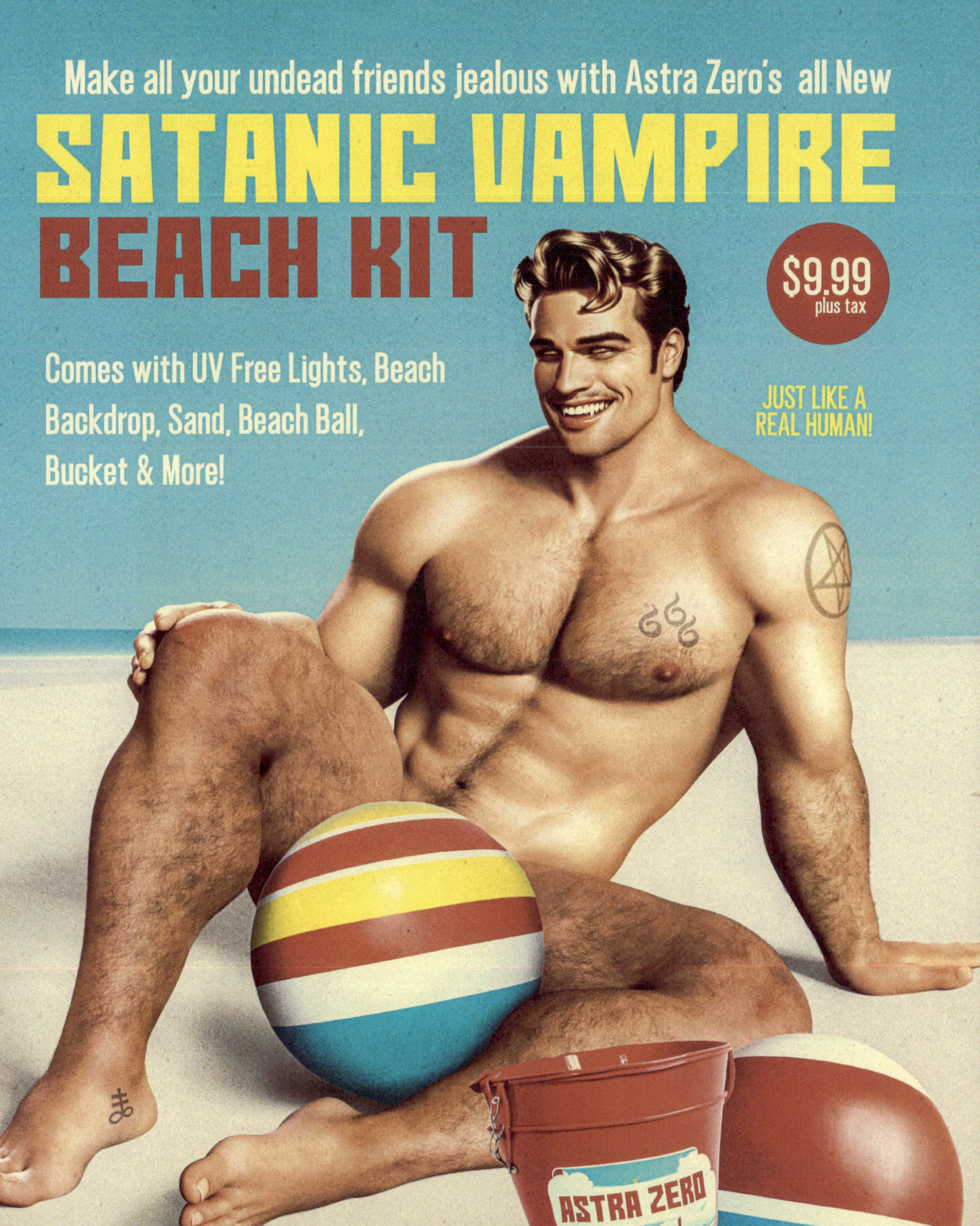

Make all your undead friends jealous with Astra Zero's all New
SATANIC VAMPIRE
BEACH KIT
$9.99
plus tax
Comes with UV Free Lights, Beach
Backdrop, Sand, Beach Ball,
Bucket & More!
JUST LIKE A
REAL HUMAN!
ASTRA ZERO

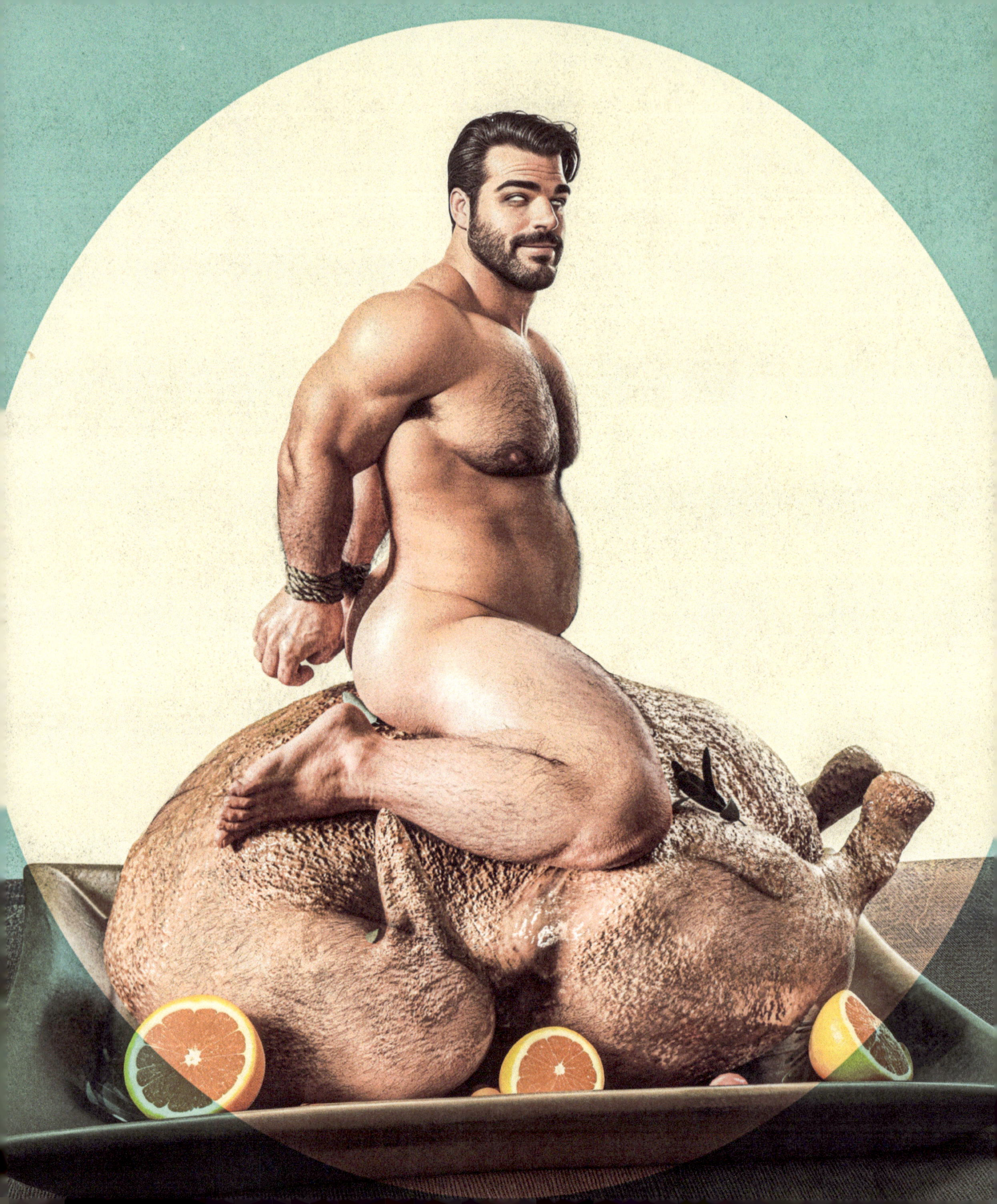

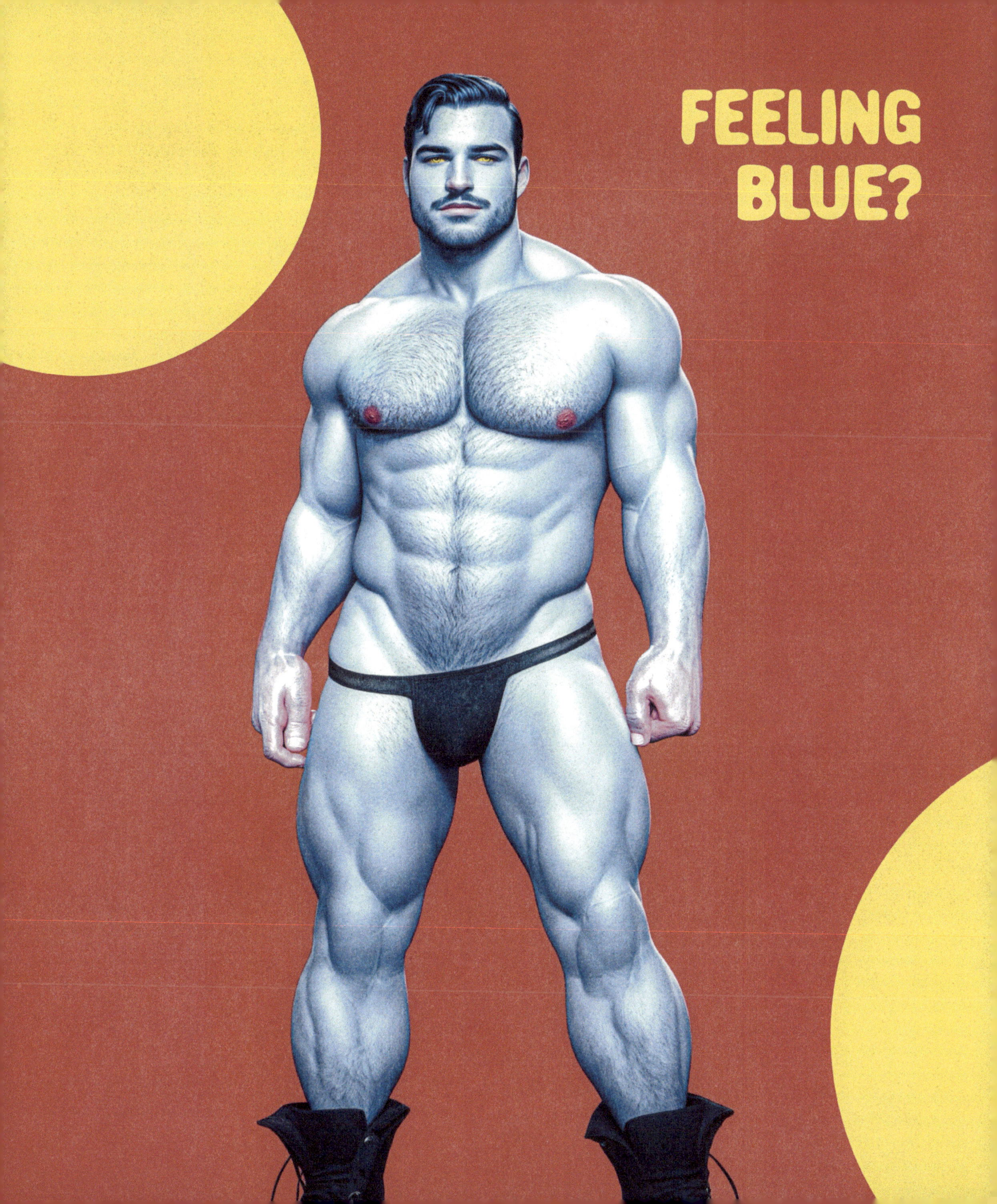

FEELING
BLUE?

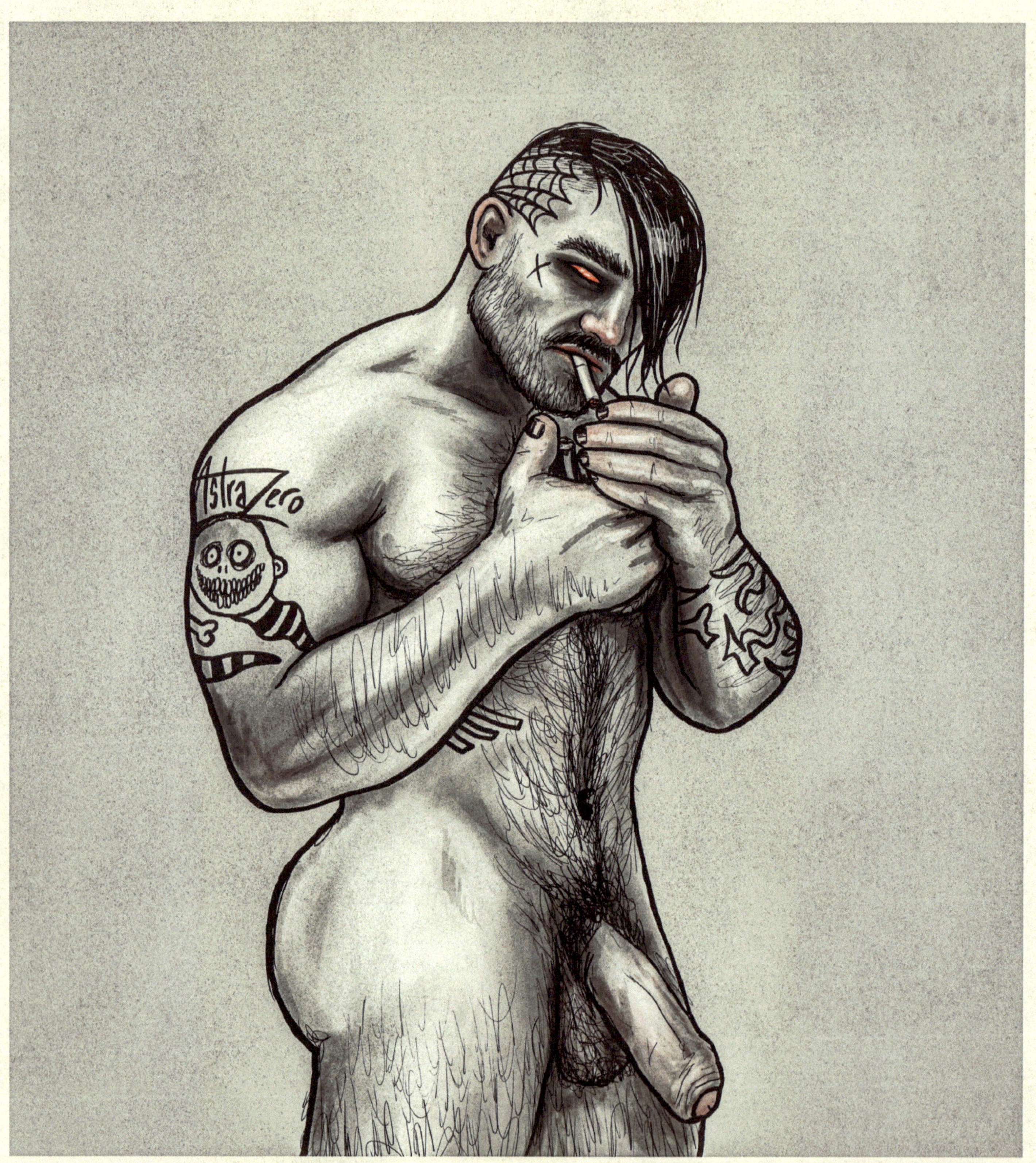
AstraZero

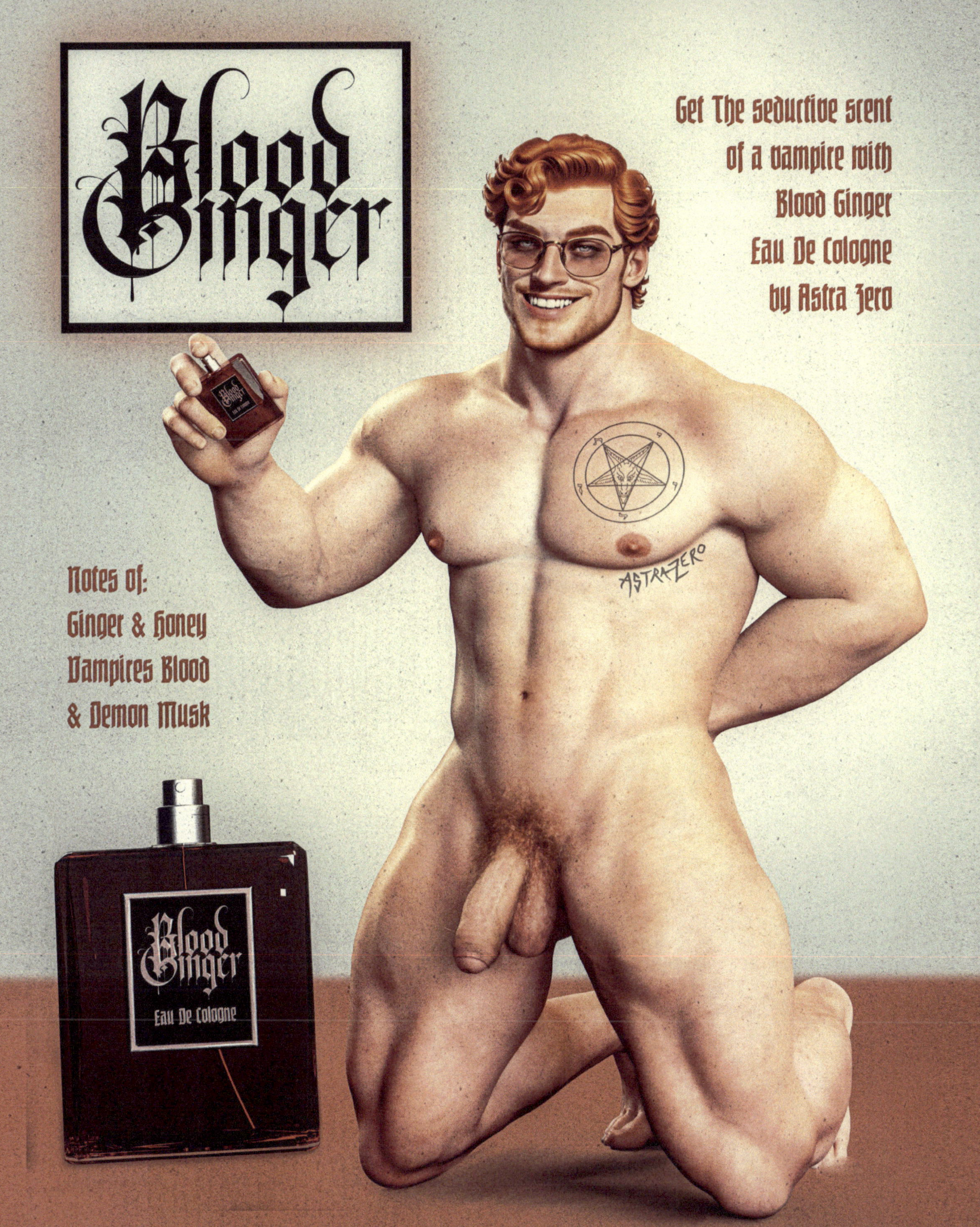

Blood Ginger
Get the seductive scent of a vampire with Blood Ginger Eau De Cologne by Astra Zero
AstraZero
Notes of:
Ginger & Honey
Vampires Blood
& Demon Musk
Blood Ginger
Eau De Cologne

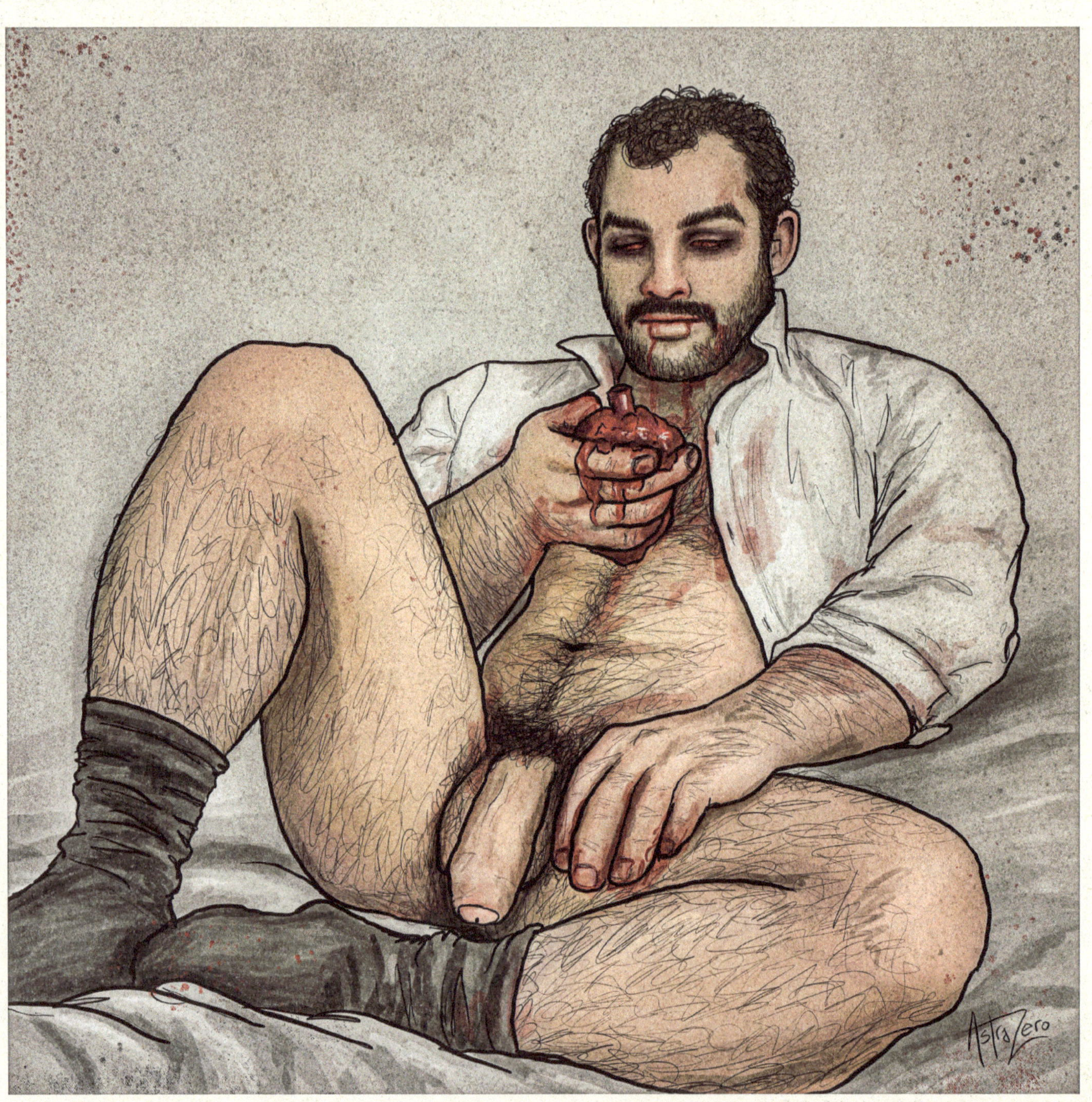

Even Jesus can't resist the great new taste of
Lucifer juice
Product of ASTRA ZERO
$666 plus tax

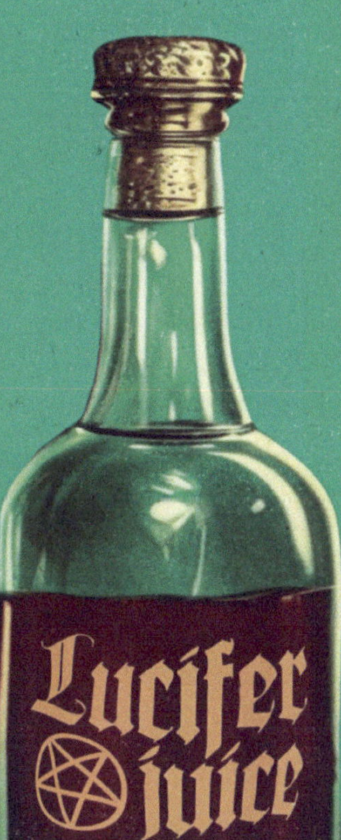

Lucifer juice

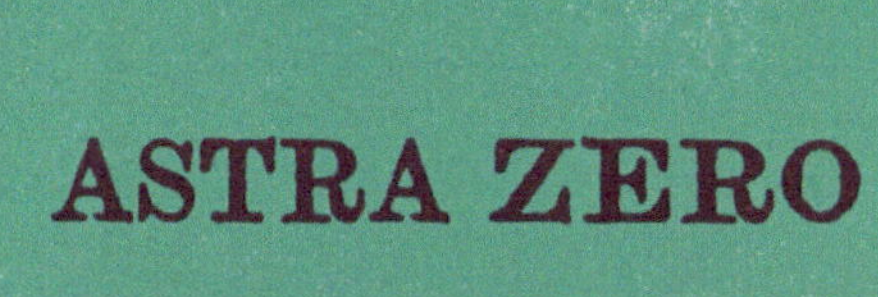

ASTRA ZERO

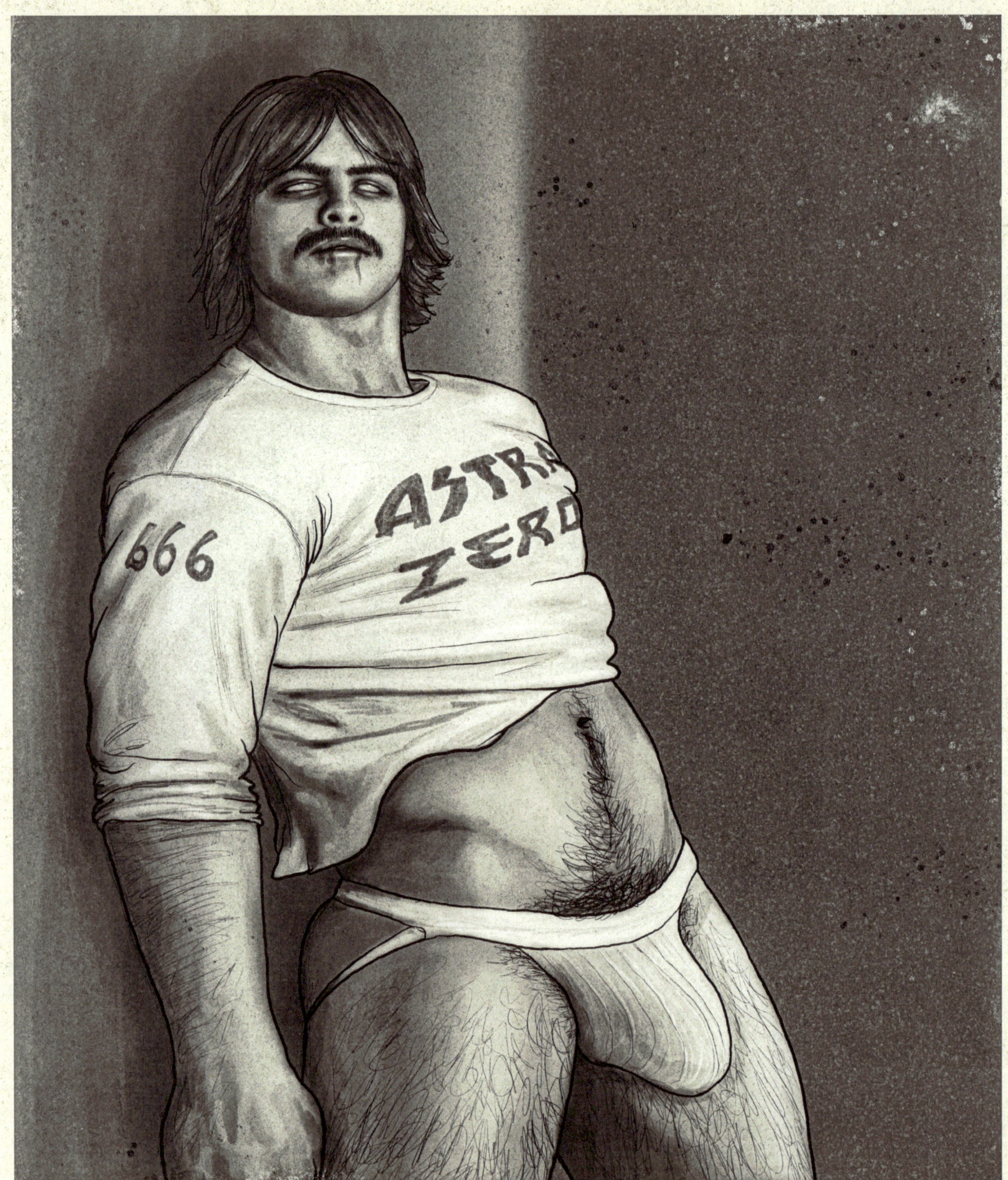

ASTRO
ZERO
666

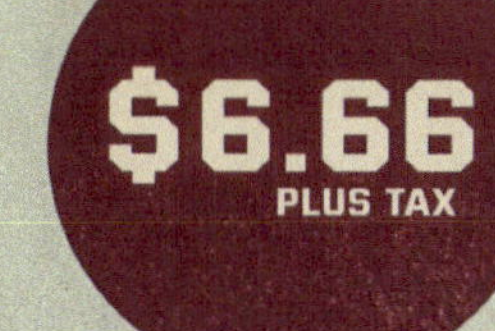

ASTRA ZERO'S
BloodLust
COFFEE
$6.66
PLUS TAX
BloodLust
COFFEE
Real taste of blood
in every cup!
ASTRA ZERO'S
BloodLust
COFFEE
A SINNERS DREAM
REAL TASTE OF BLOOD IN EVERY CUP
Blood Soaked
Ground Coffee

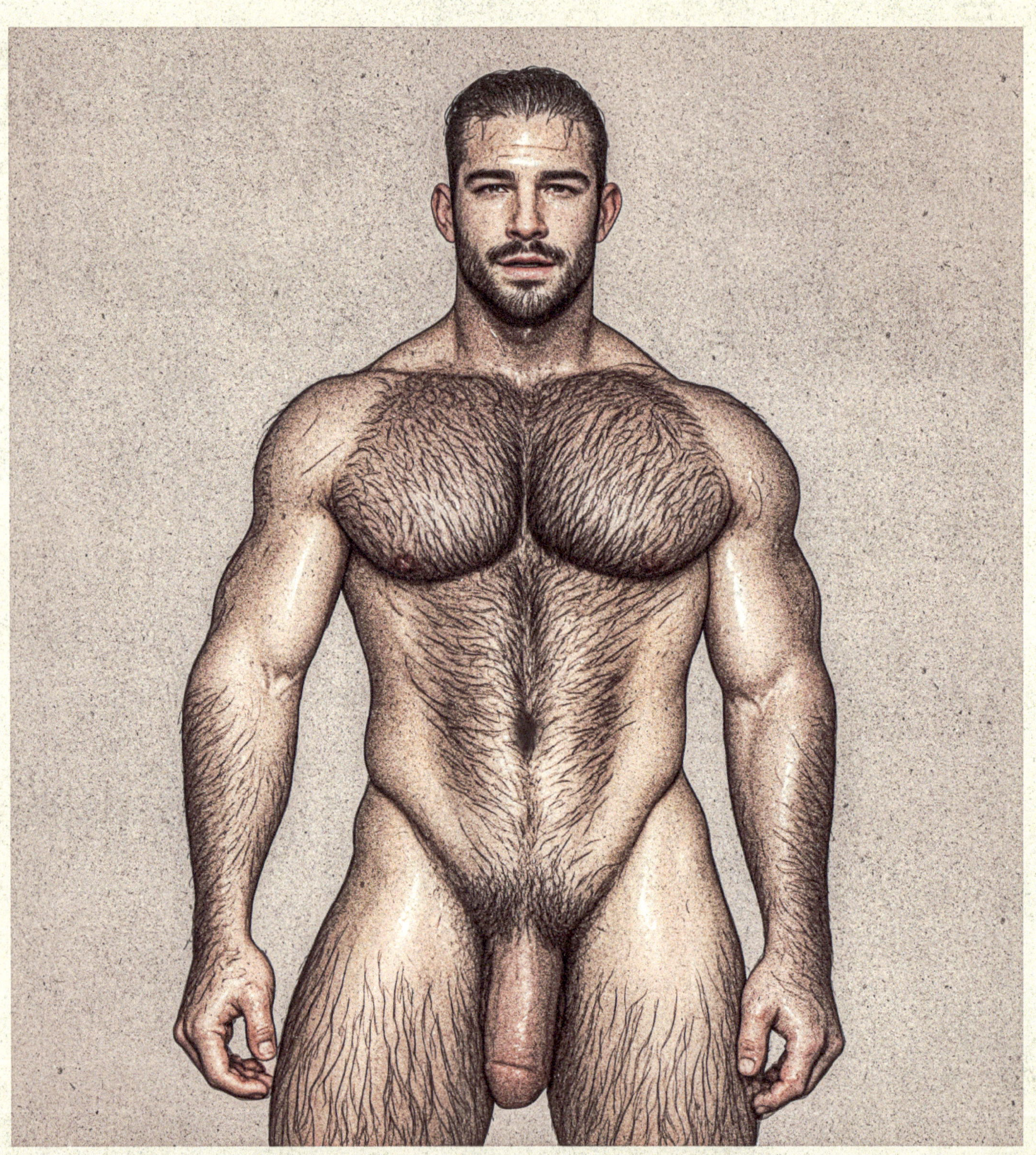

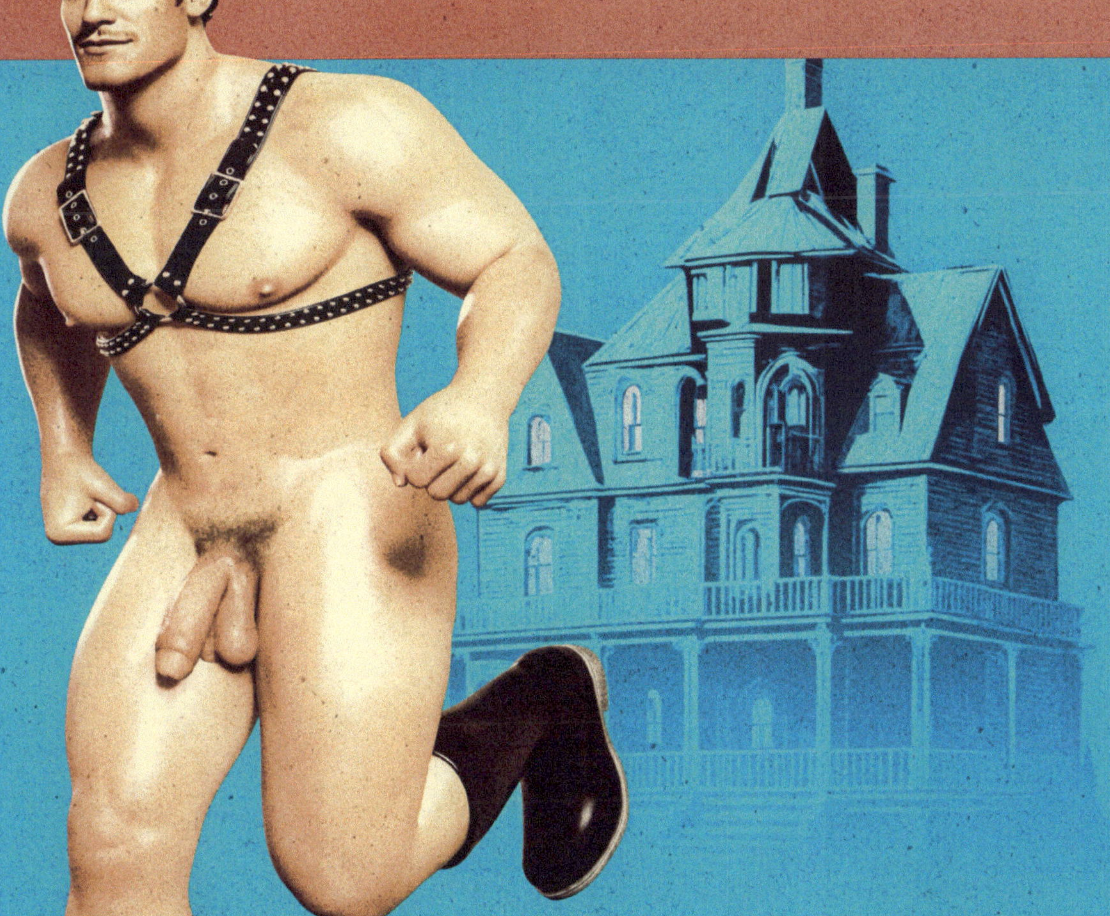

MYSTERY OF THE MISSING PANTS
AZ
SHOCKING!
THRILLING!
SEXY & CLEVER!

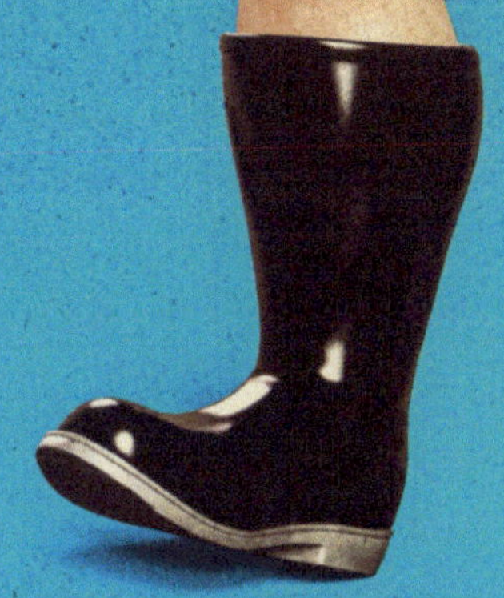

WRITTEN BY:
ASTRA ZERO
SATANIC CULT BEST SELLER!
666 XXX 0010
69¢ PLUS TAX

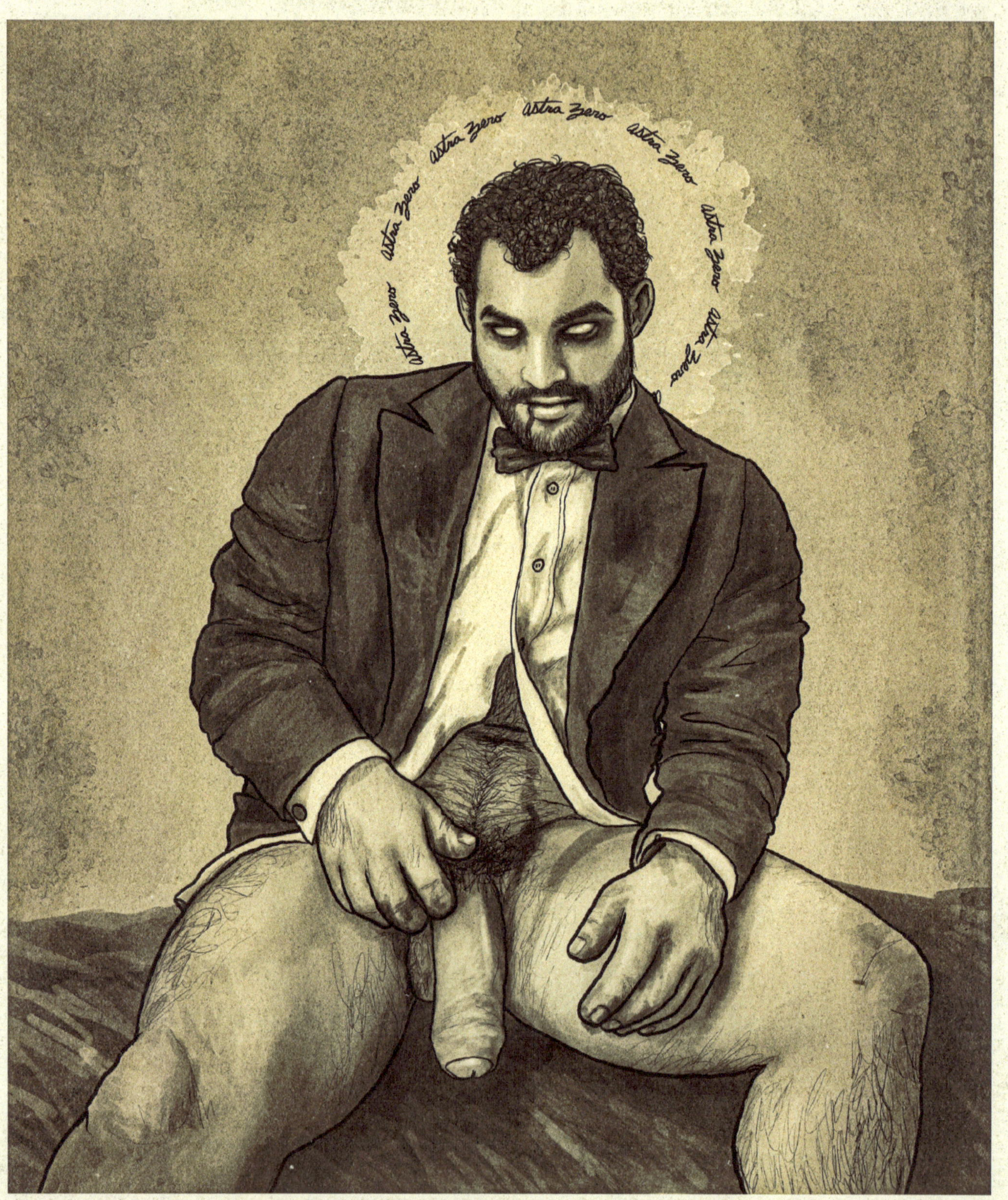
Astra Zero
Astra Zero
Astra Zero
Astra Zero
Astra Zero
Astra Zero
Astra Zero
Astra Zero

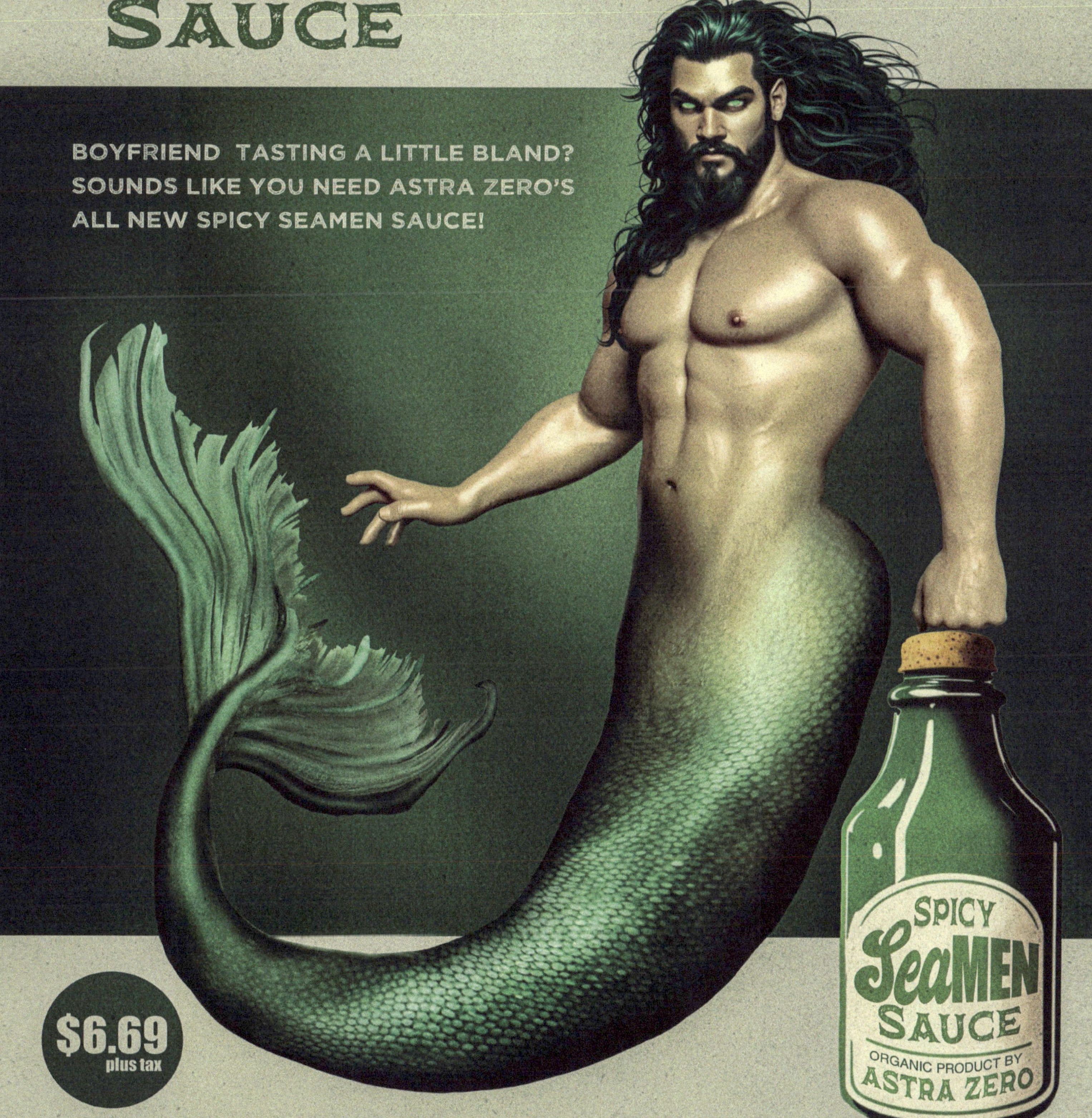
SPICY
SeaMEN
SAUCE
MADE FROM / BY REAL MERMEN
100% ORGANIC
BOYFRIEND TASTING A LITTLE BLAND?
SOUNDS LIKE YOU NEED ASTRA ZERO'S
ALL NEW SPICY SEAMEN SAUCE!
$6.69
plus tax
SPICY
SeaMEN
SAUCE
ORGANIC PRODUCT BY
ASTRA ZERO

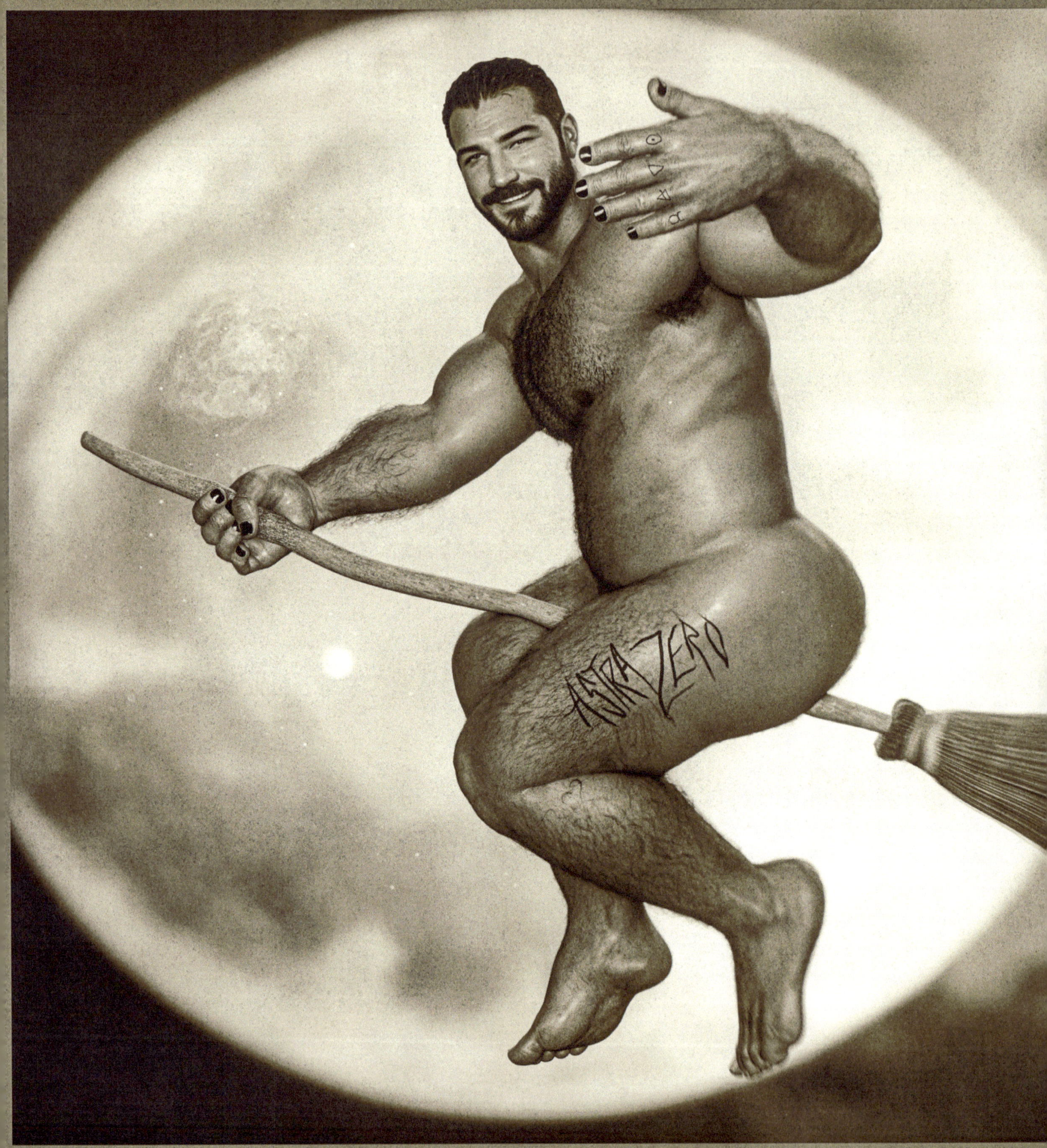
ASTRA ZERO

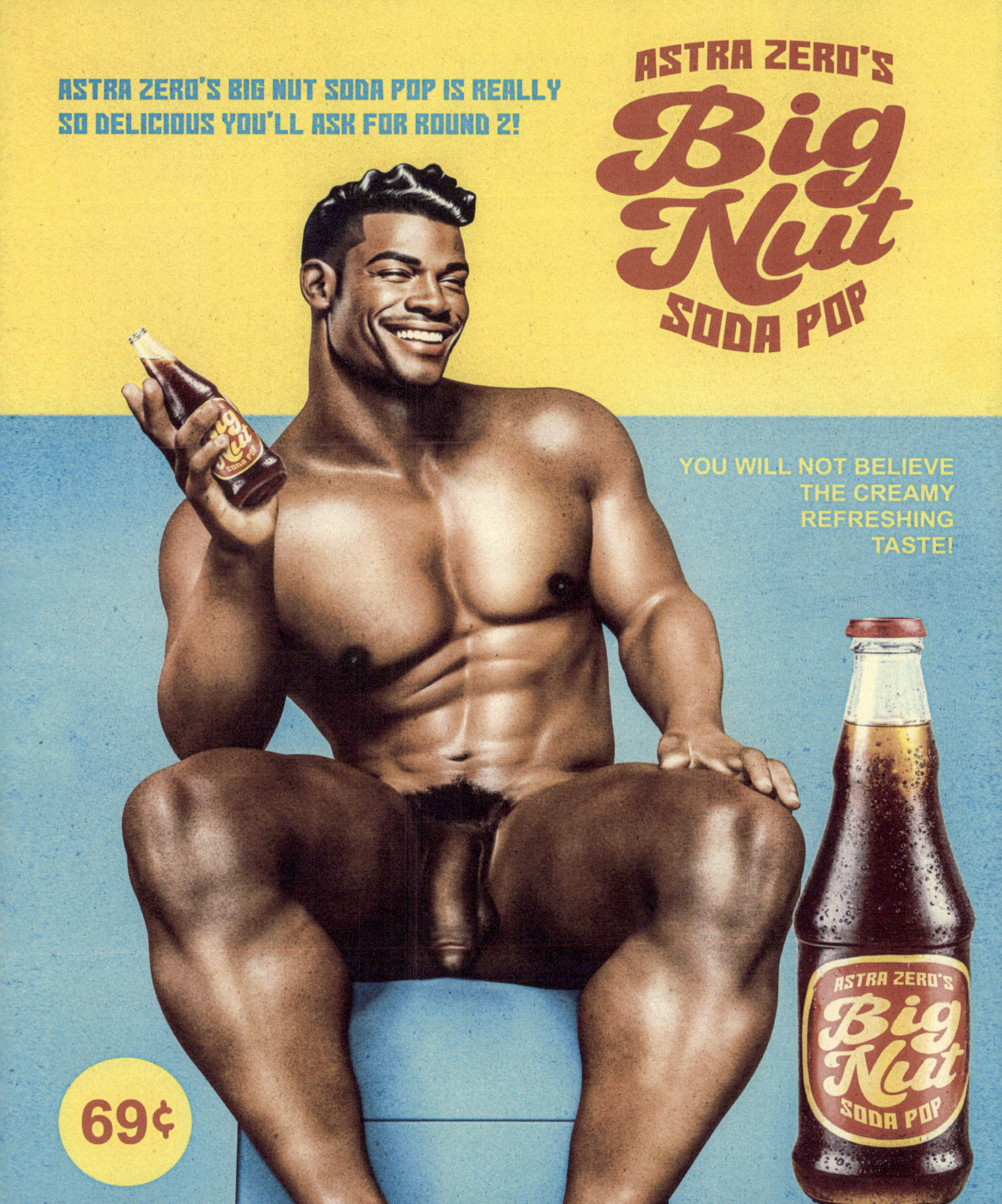

ASTRA ZERO'S BIG NUT SODA POP IS REALLY SO DELICIOUS YOU'LL ASK FOR ROUND 2!
ASTRA ZERO'S
Big Nut
SODA POP
YOU WILL NOT BELIEVE THE CREAMY REFRESHING TASTE!
69¢
ASTRA ZERO'S
Big Nut
SODA POP

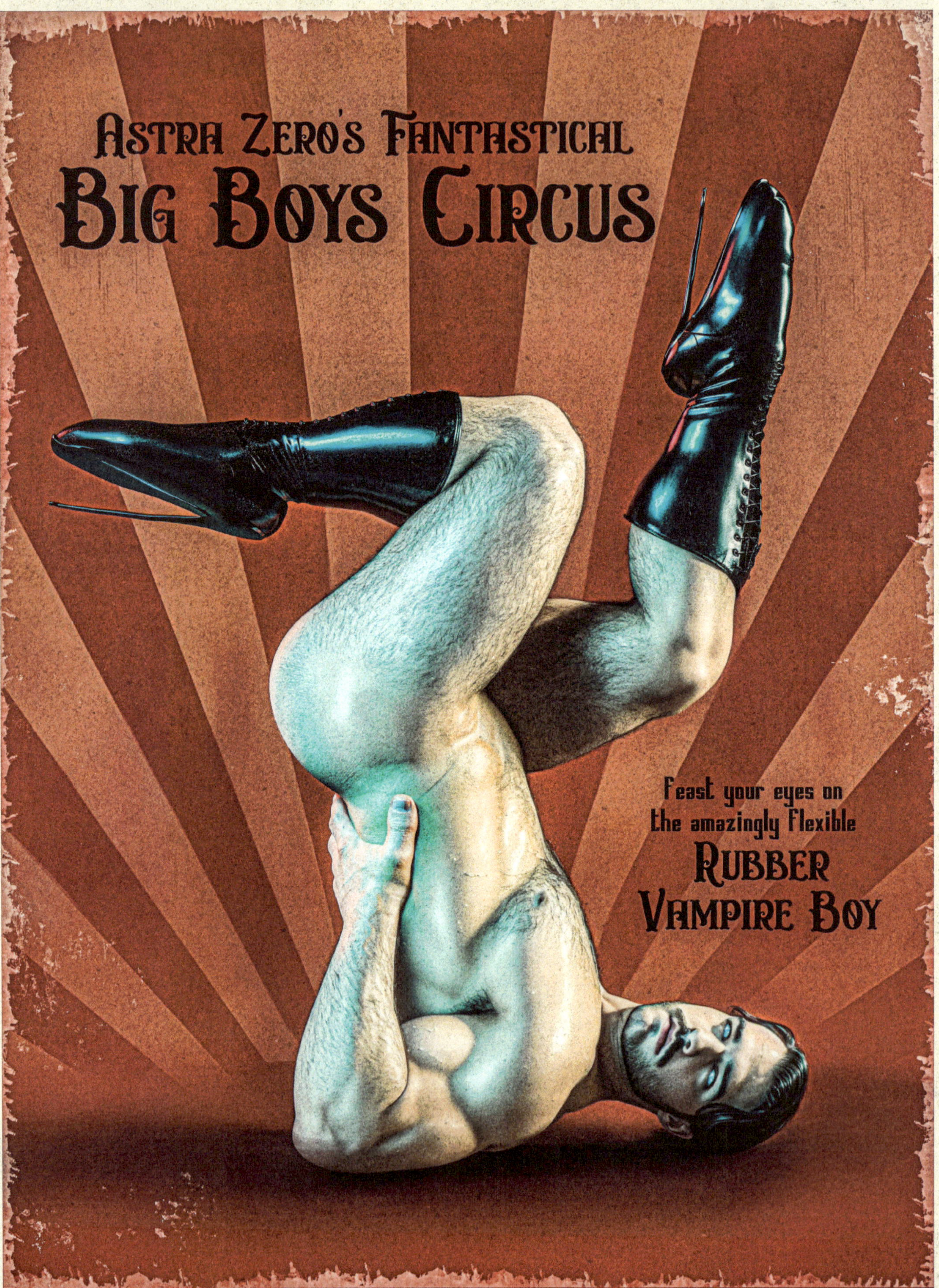

Astra Zero's Fantastical
Big Boys Circus
Feast your eyes on
the amazingly flexible
Rubber
Vampire Boy

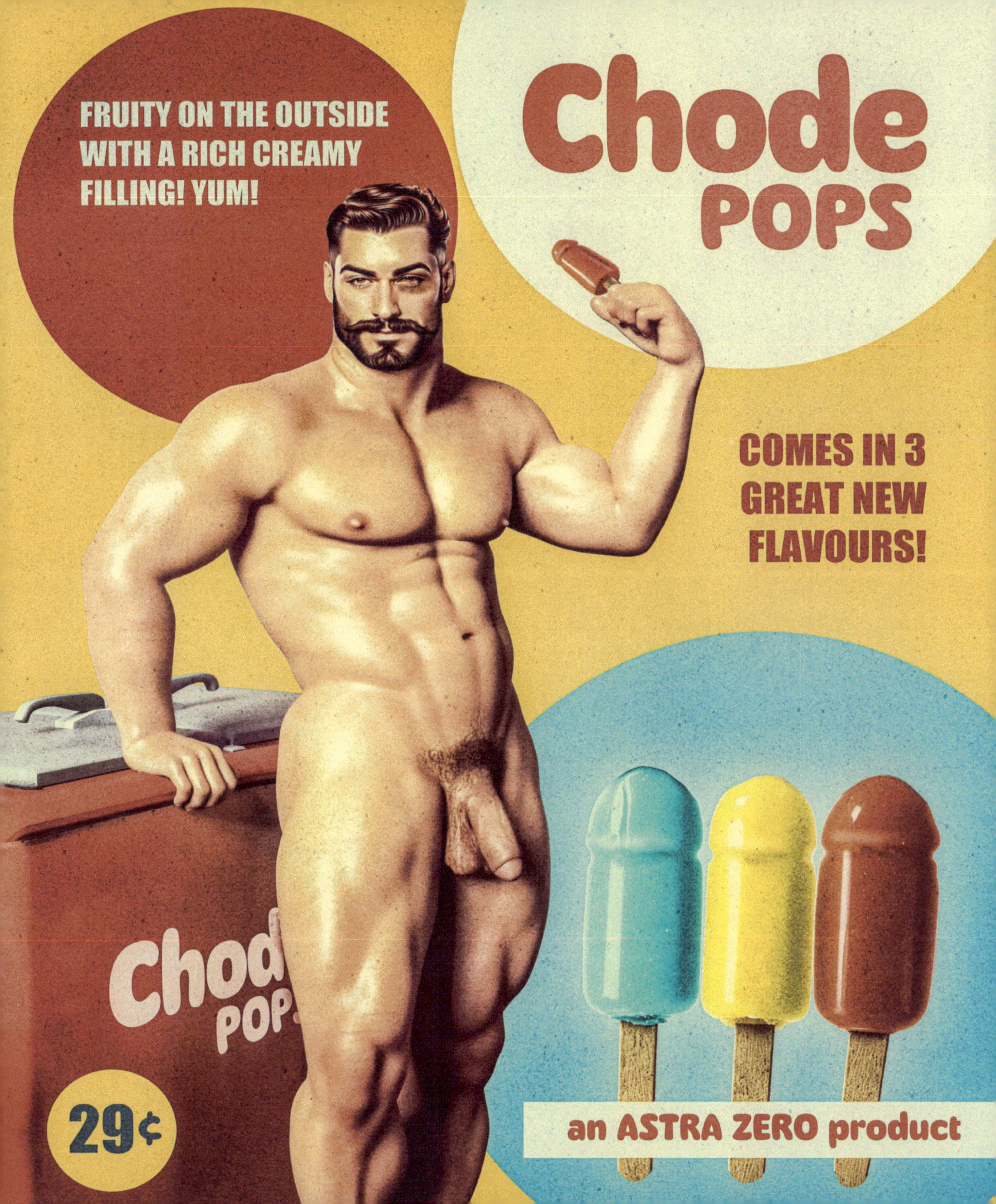

FRUITY ON THE OUTSIDE WITH A RICH CREAMY FILLING! YUM!
Chode
POPS
COMES IN 3 GREAT NEW FLAVOURS!
Chode POPS
29¢
an ASTRA ZERO product

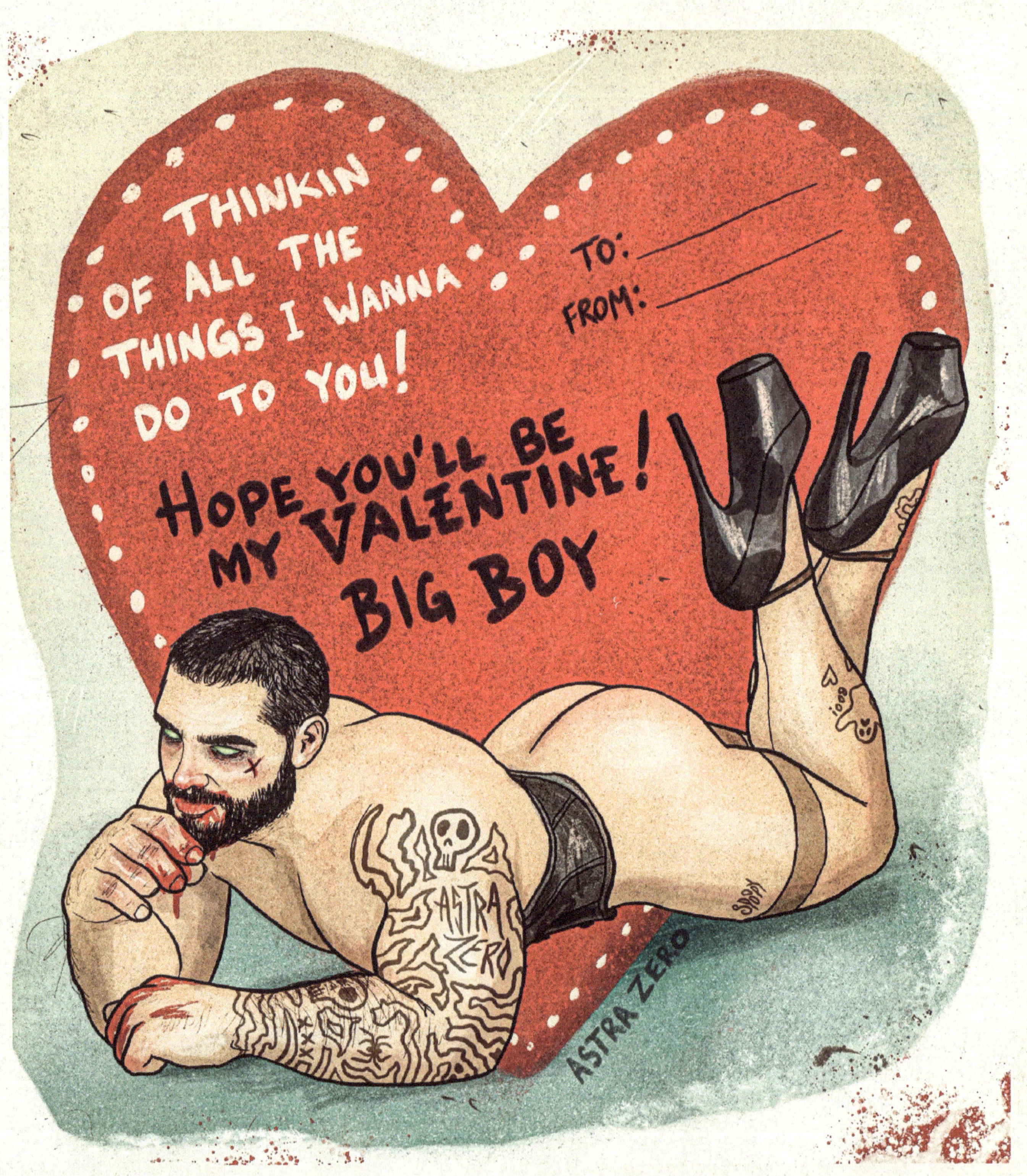

THINKIN OF ALL THE THINGS I WANNA DO TO YOU!
TO: ____
FROM: ____
HOPE YOU'LL BE MY VALENTINE! BIG BOY
ASTRA ZERO
ASTRA ZERO

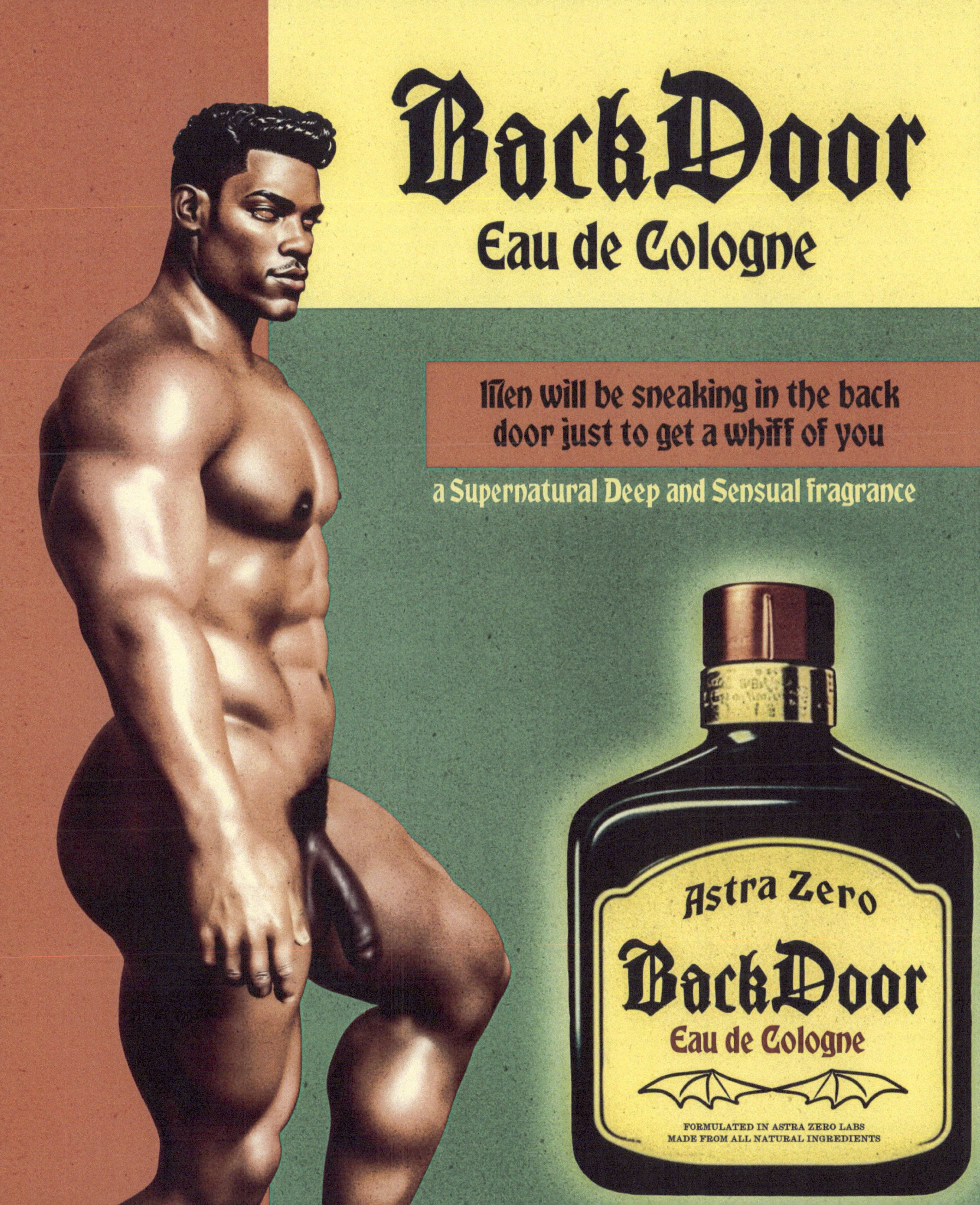

BackDoor
Eau de Cologne
Men will be sneaking in the back door just to get a whiff of you
a Supernatural Deep and Sensual fragrance
Astra Zero
BackDoor
Eau de Cologne
FORMULATED IN ASTRA ZERO LABS
MADE FROM ALL NATURAL INGREDIENTS

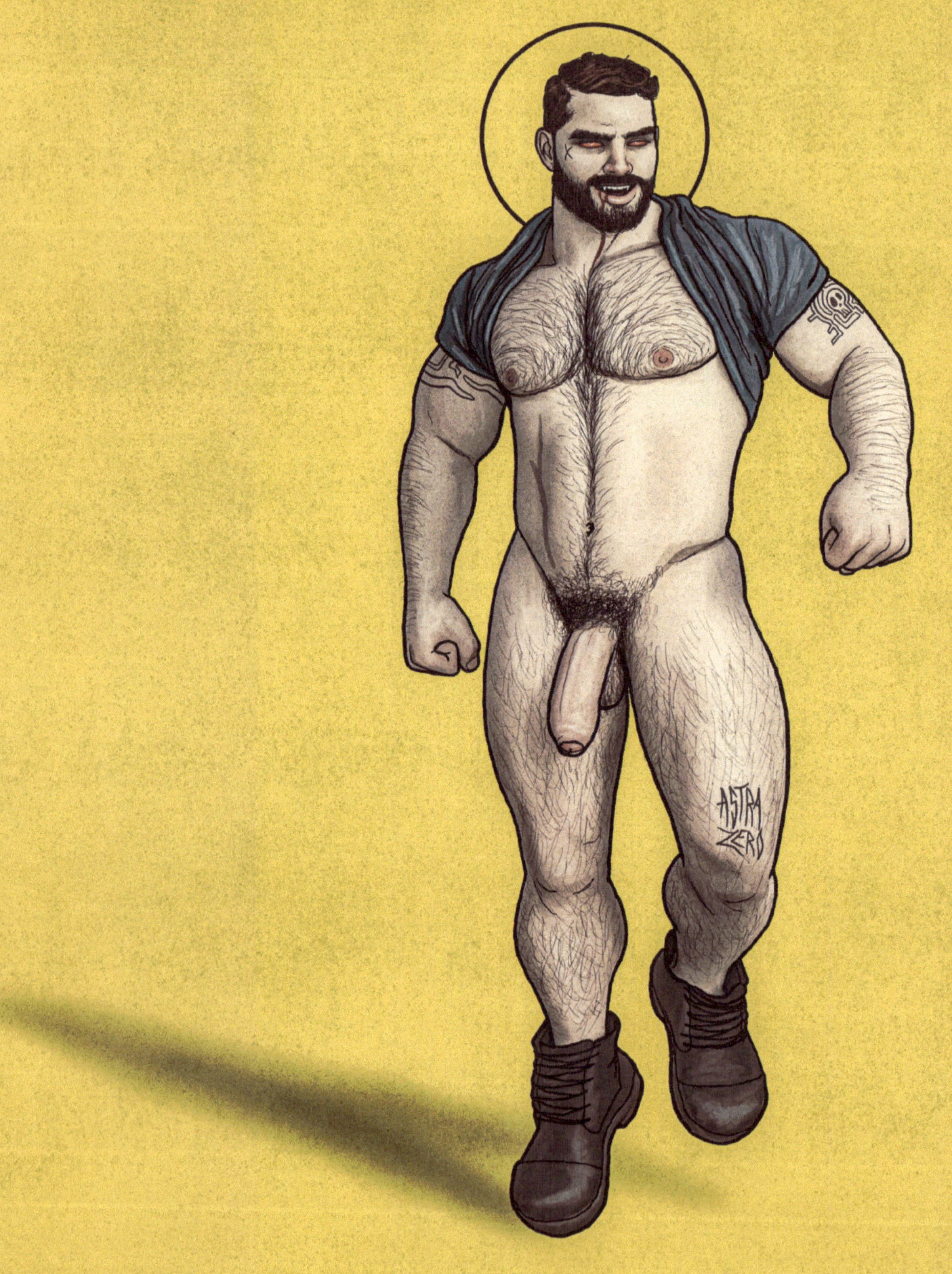

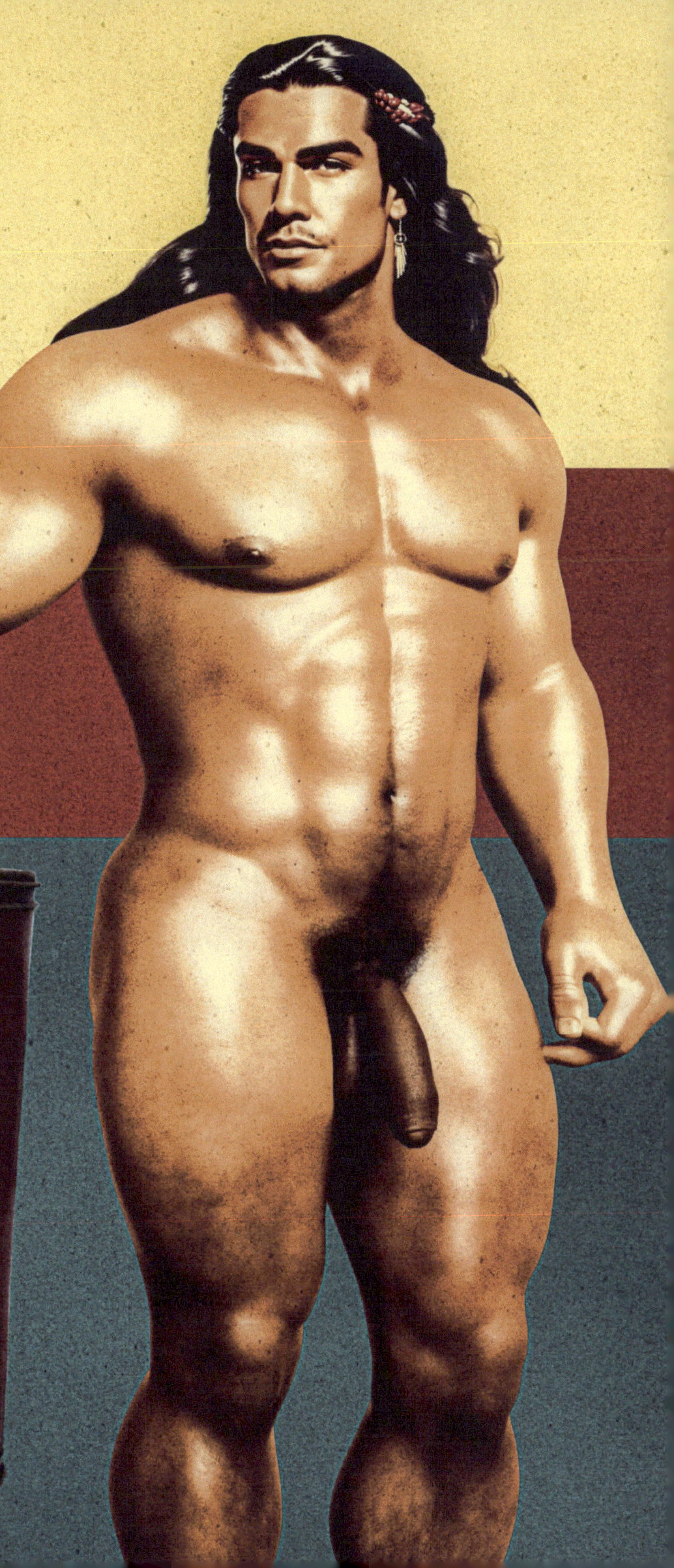

Stiff
BEAR
TOBACCO
Smooth
Rich
Earthy
Flavour
ASTRA ZERO
Stiff
BEAR
TOBACCO
666 XXX 666

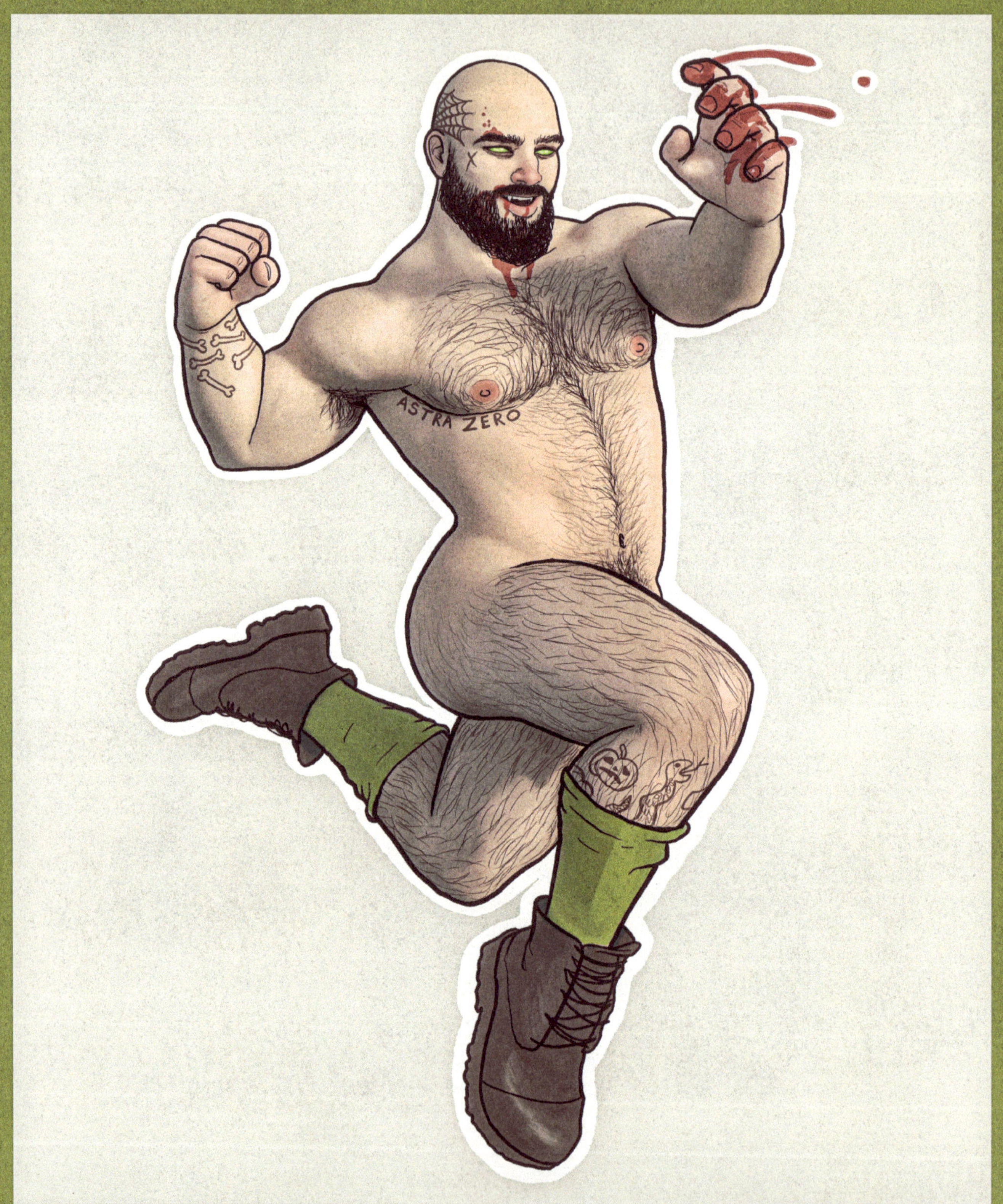

ASTRA ZERO

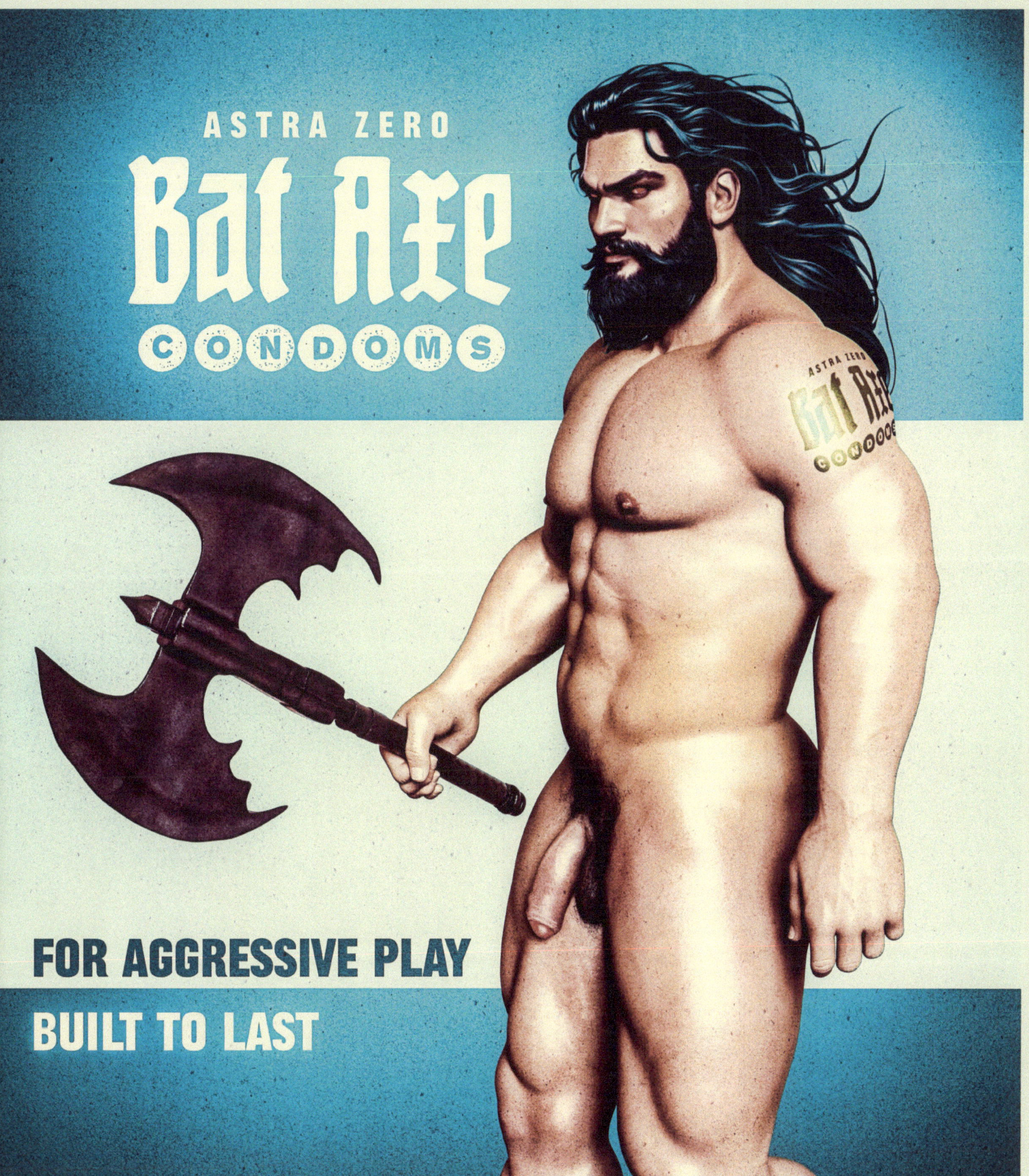

ASTRA ZERO
Bat Axe
CONDOMS
FOR AGGRESSIVE PLAY
BUILT TO LAST
ASTRA ZERO
Bat Axe
CONDOMS

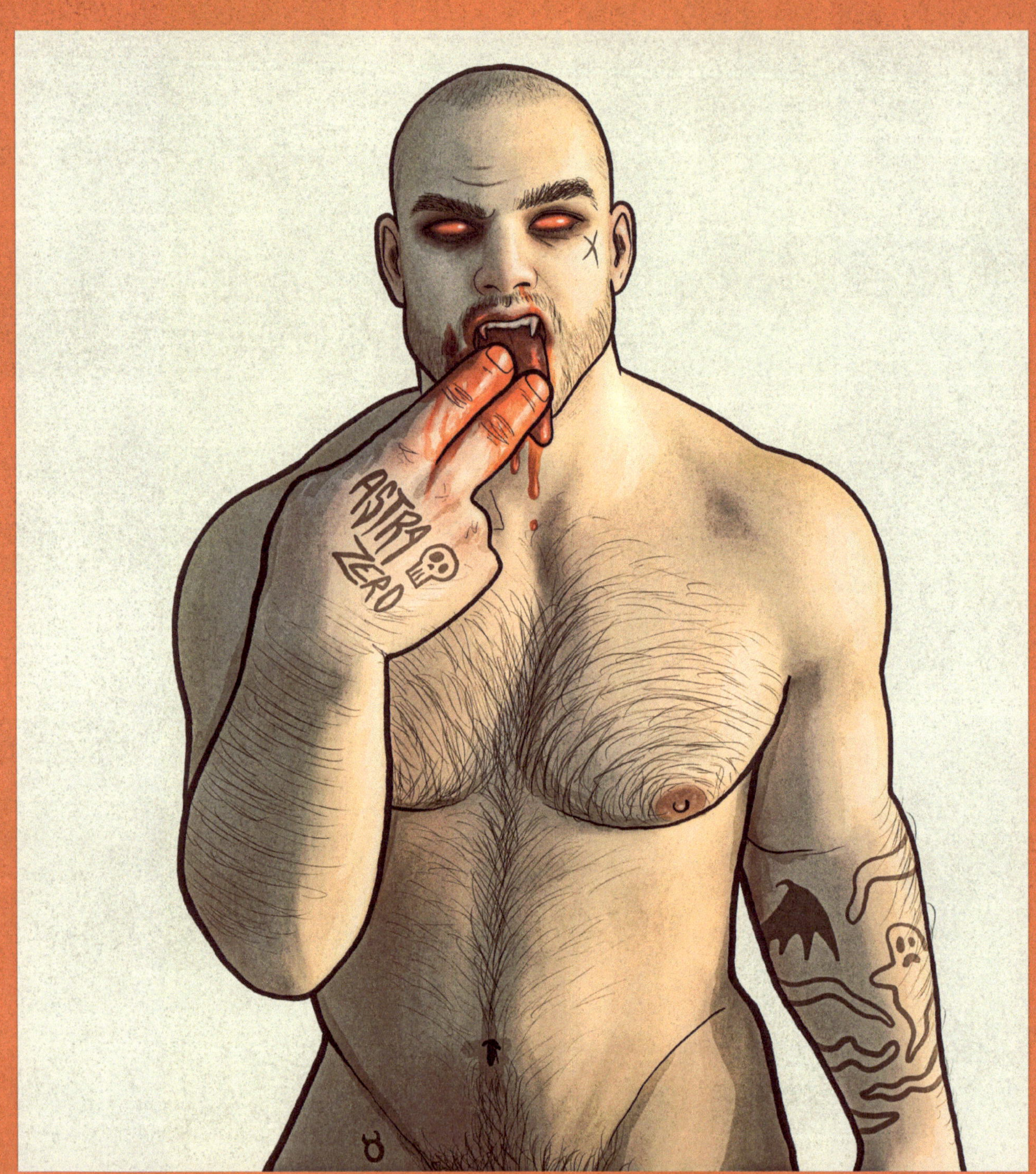

ASTRA
ZERO

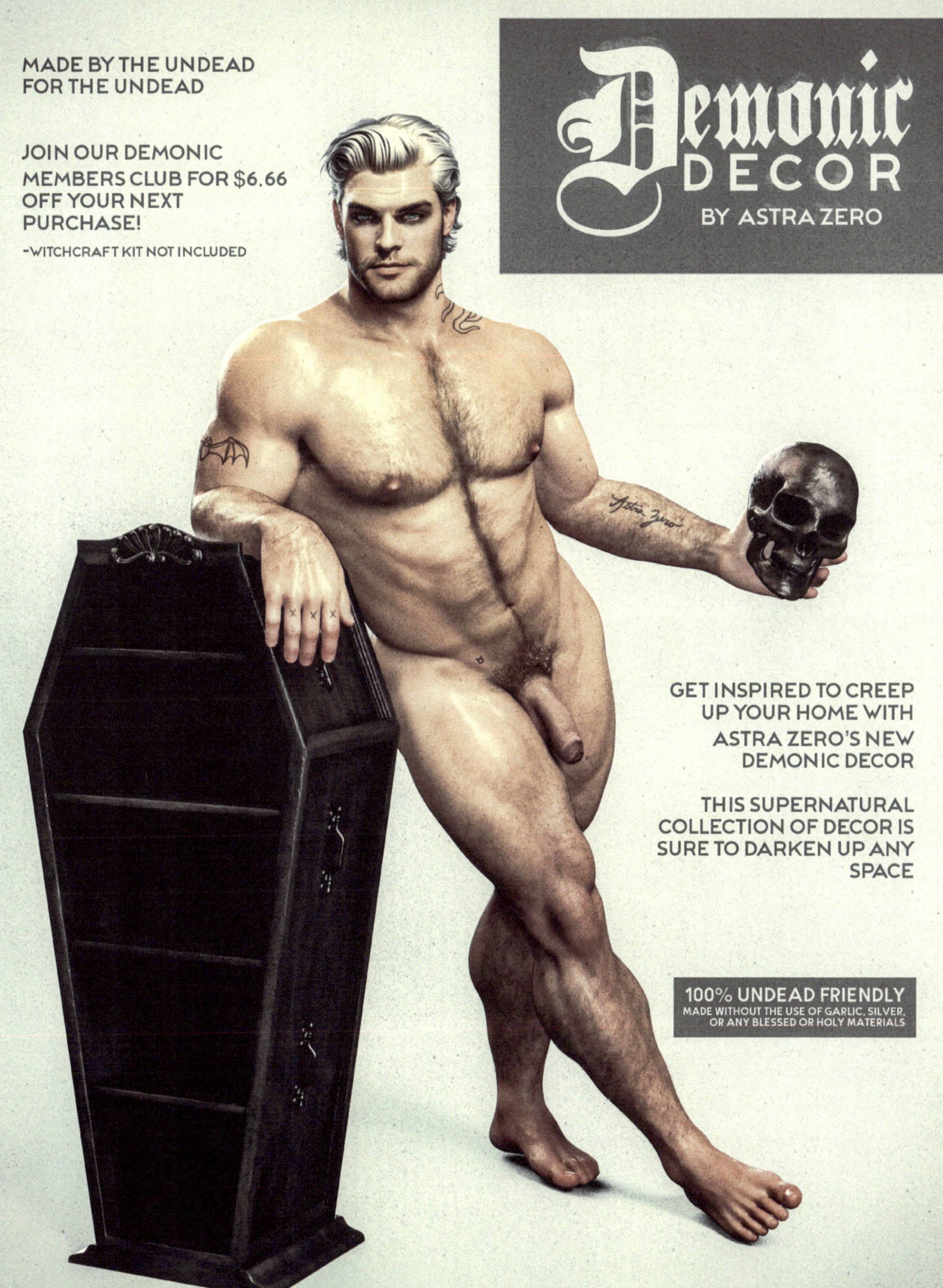
MADE BY THE UNDEAD
FOR THE UNDEAD

JOIN OUR DEMONIC
MEMBERS CLUB FOR $6.66
OFF YOUR NEXT
PURCHASE!

-WITCHCRAFT KIT NOT INCLUDED

Demonic
DECOR
BY ASTRA ZERO

GET INSPIRED TO CREEP
UP YOUR HOME WITH
ASTRA ZERO'S NEW
DEMONIC DECOR

THIS SUPERNATURAL
COLLECTION OF DECOR IS
SURE TO DARKEN UP ANY
SPACE

100% UNDEAD FRIENDLY
MADE WITHOUT THE USE OF GARLIC, SILVER,
OR ANY BLESSED OR HOLY MATERIALS

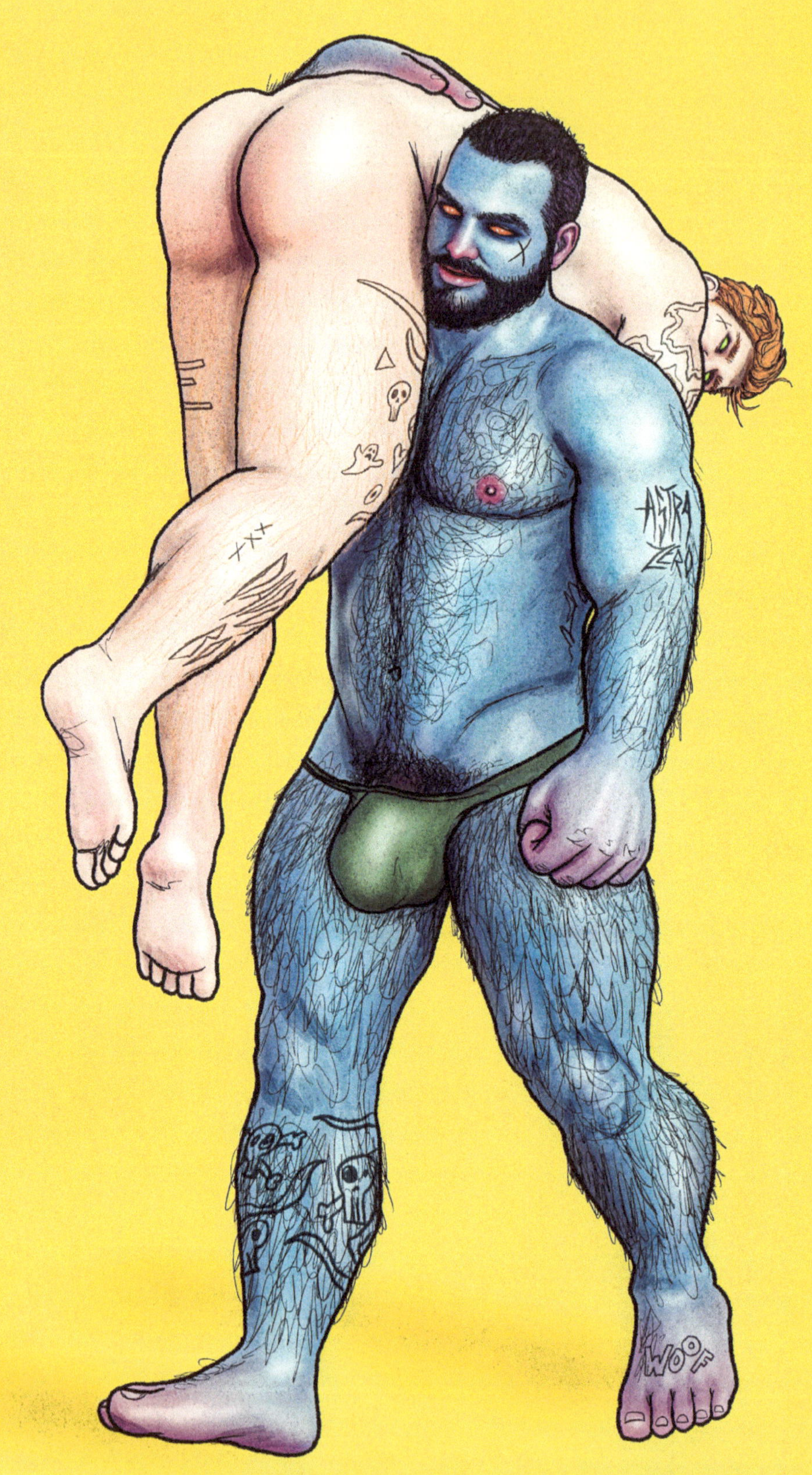

ASTRA
ZERO
WOOF

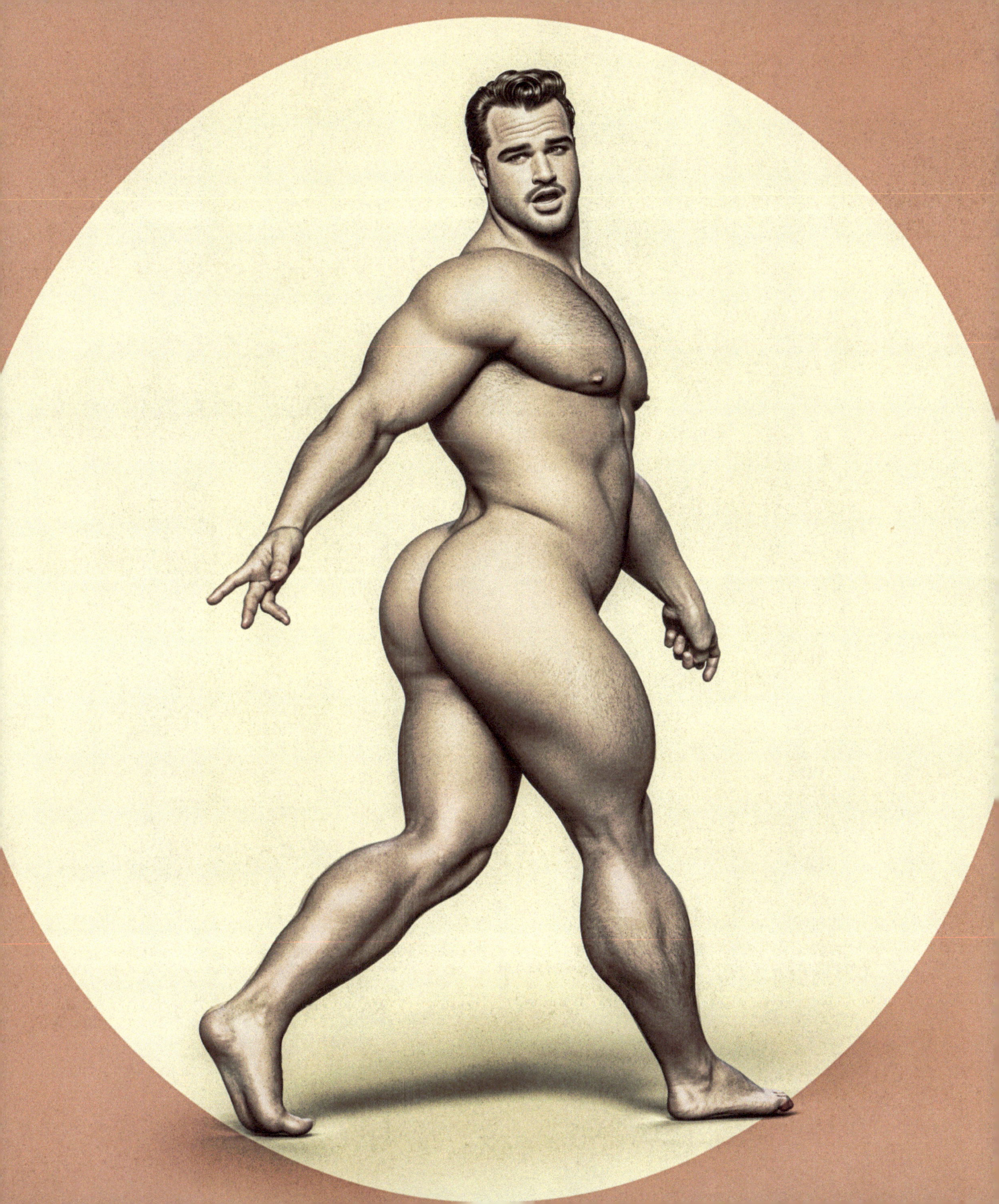

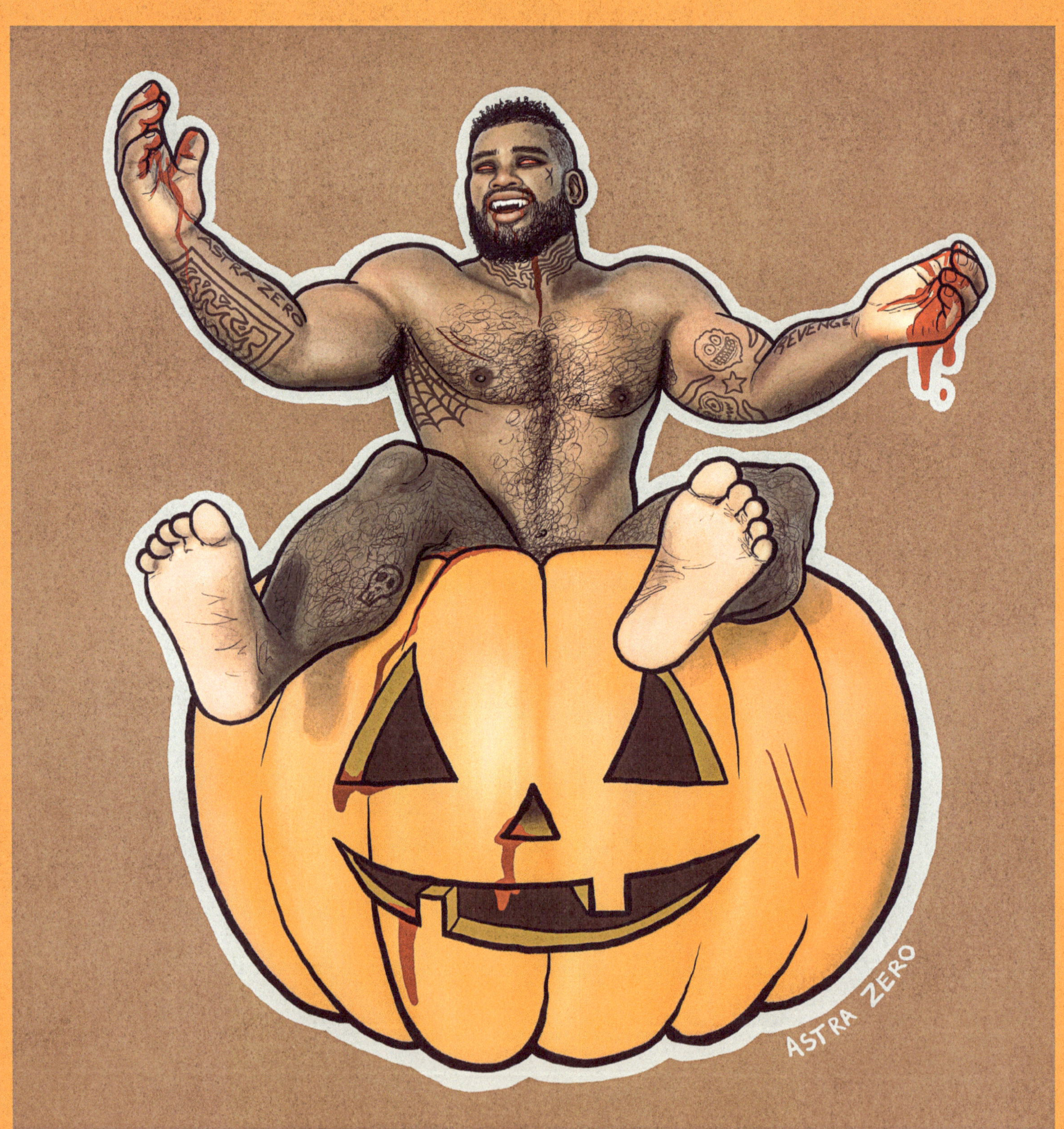
ASTRA ZERO
REVENGE
ASTRA ZERO

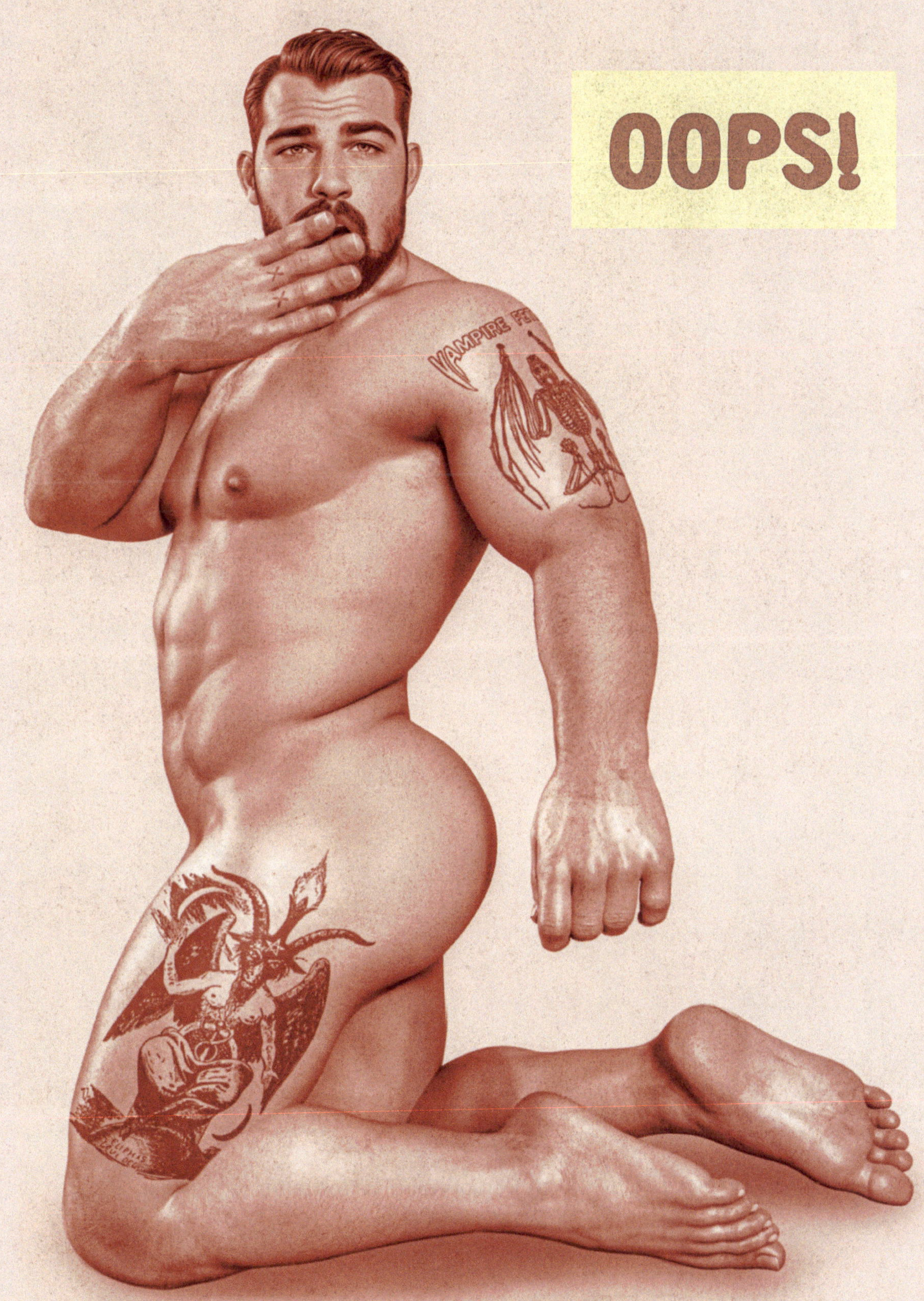
OOPS!
VAMPIRE FE

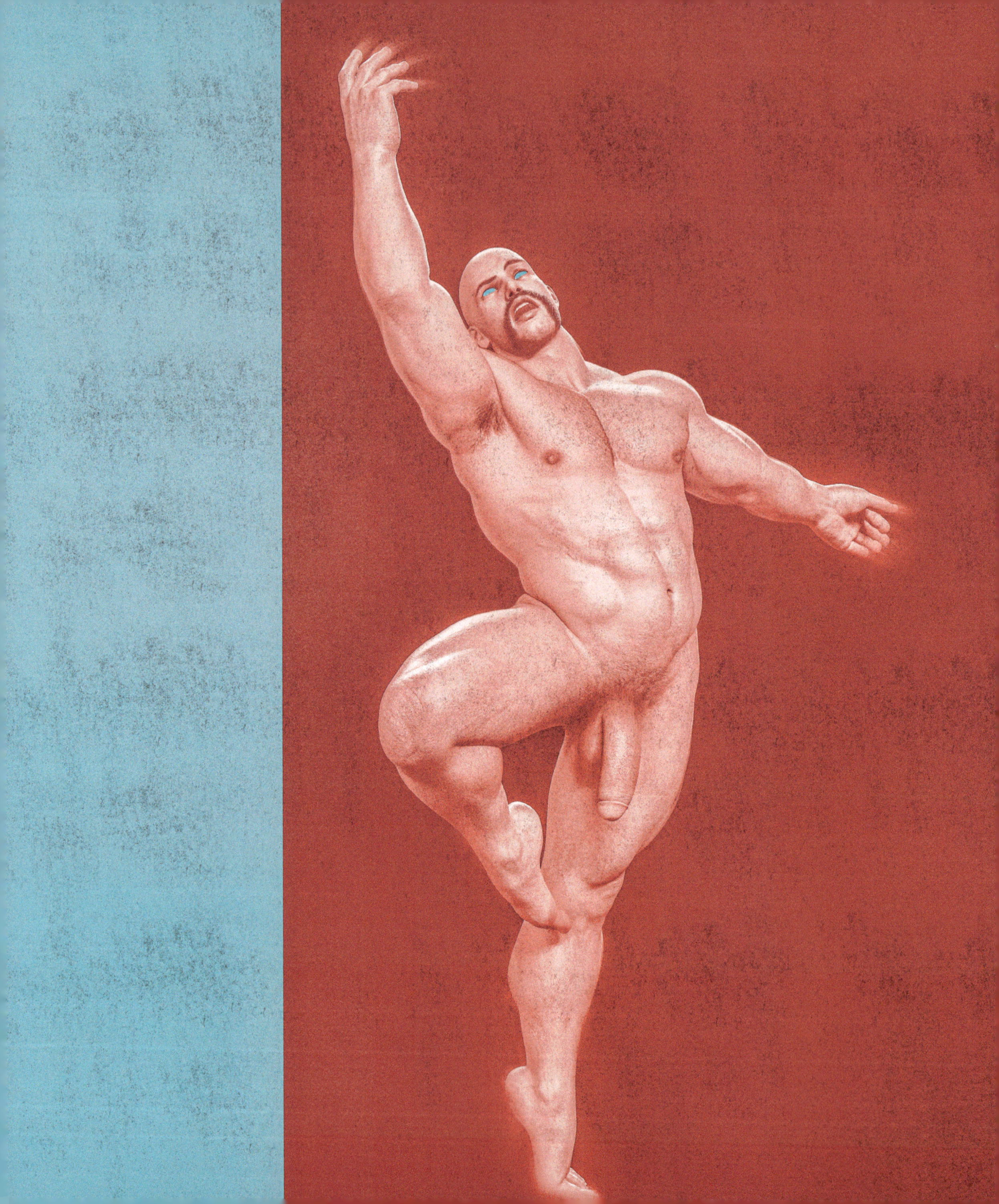

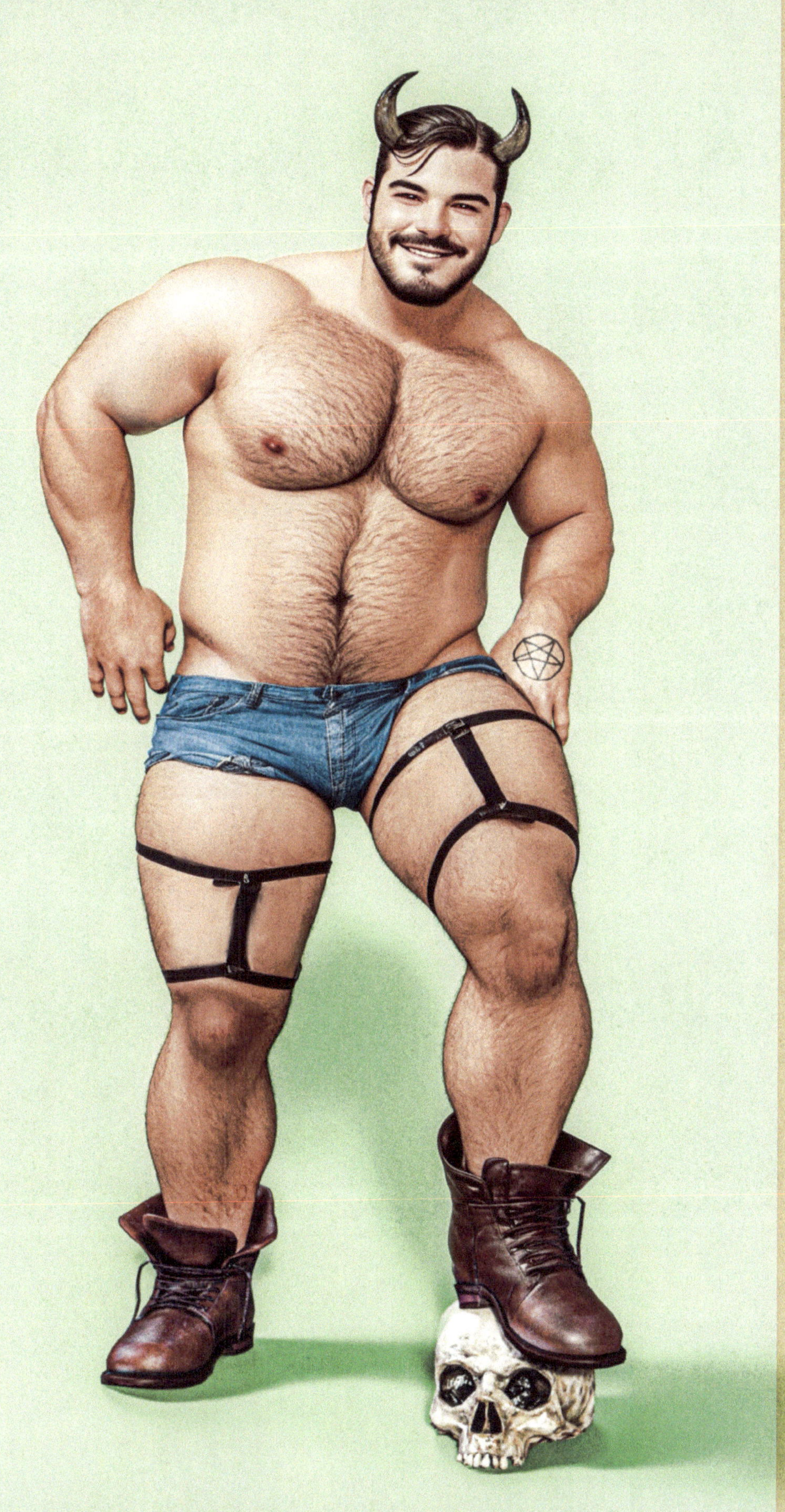

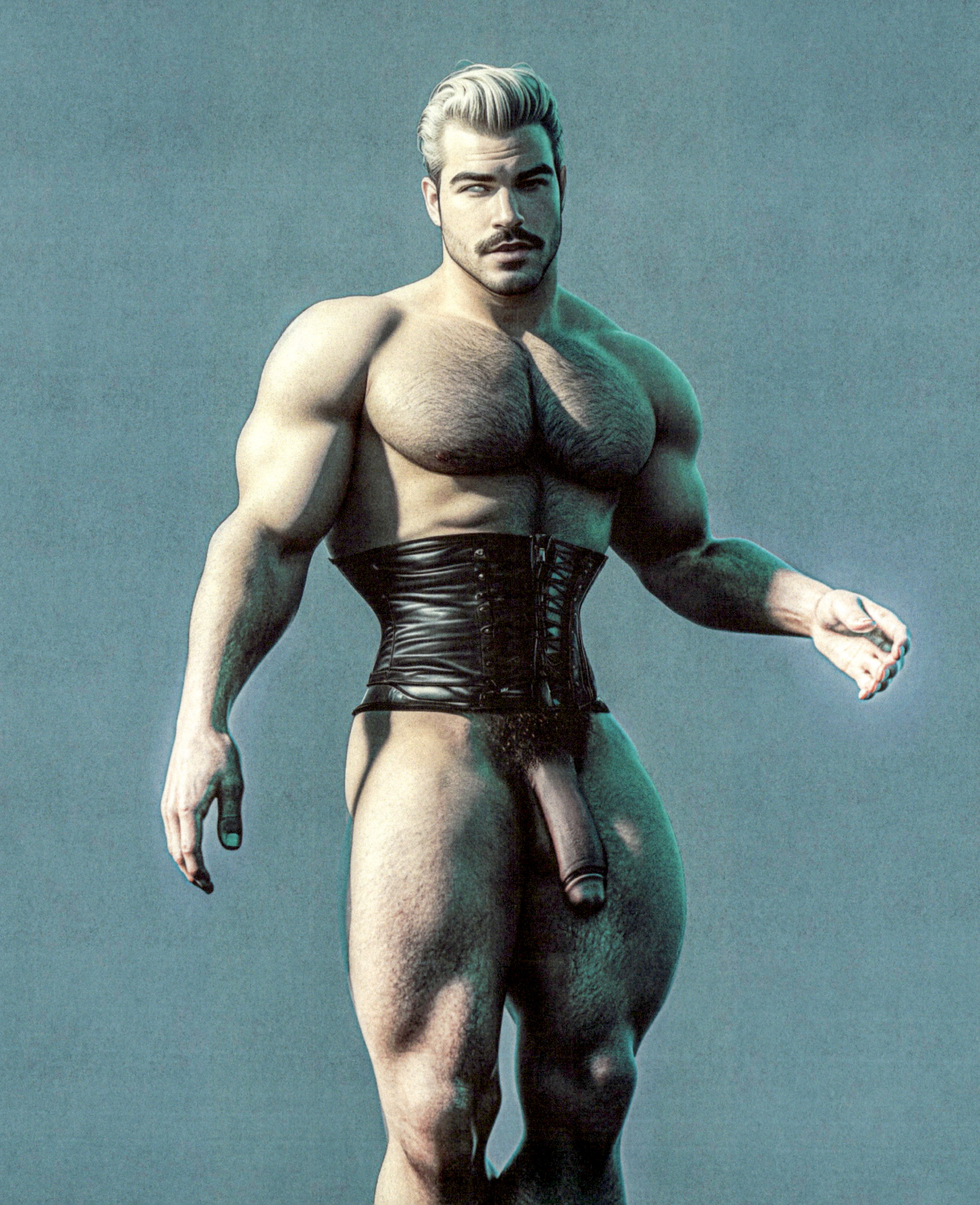

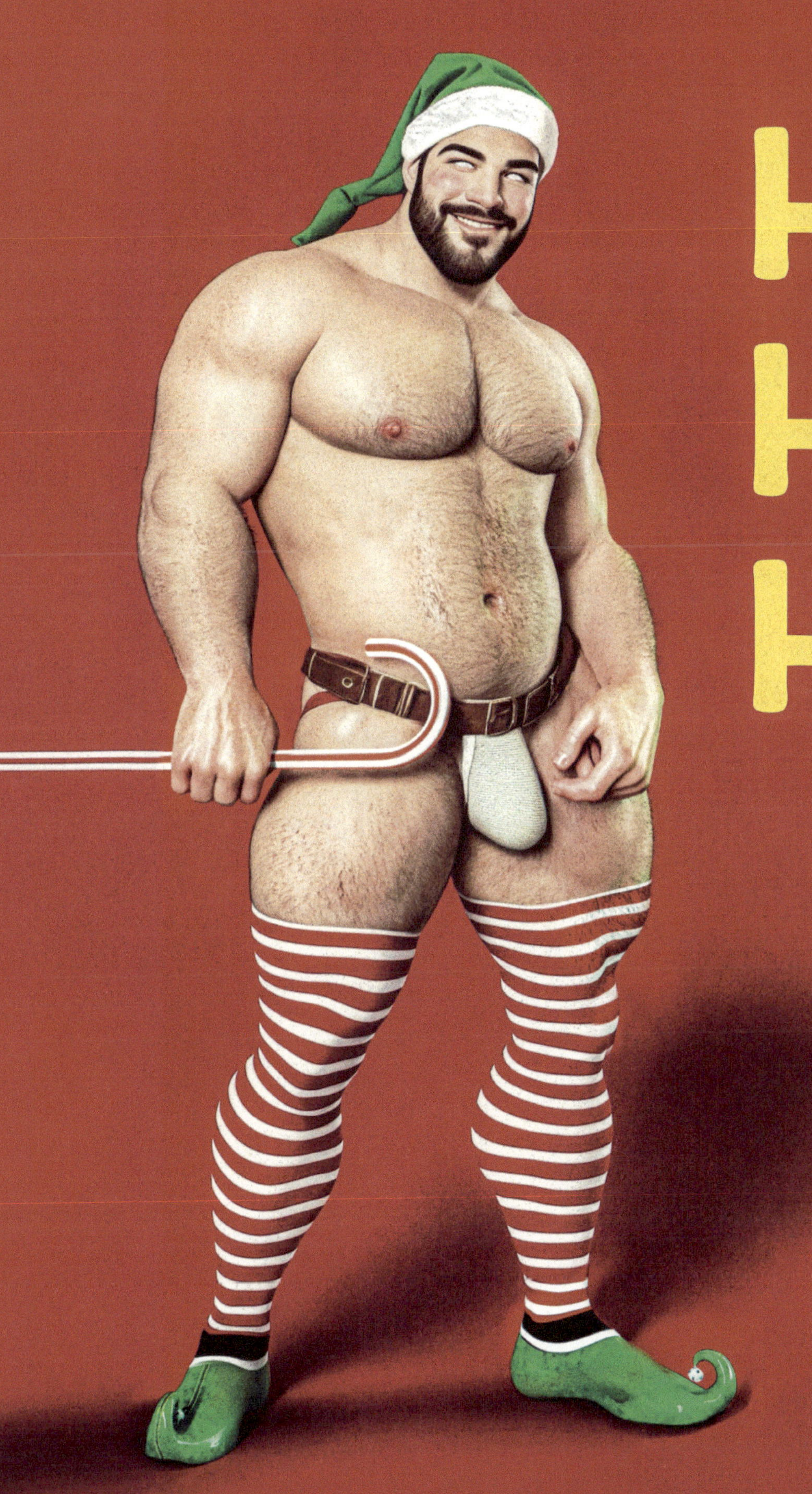

HOE
HOE
HOE

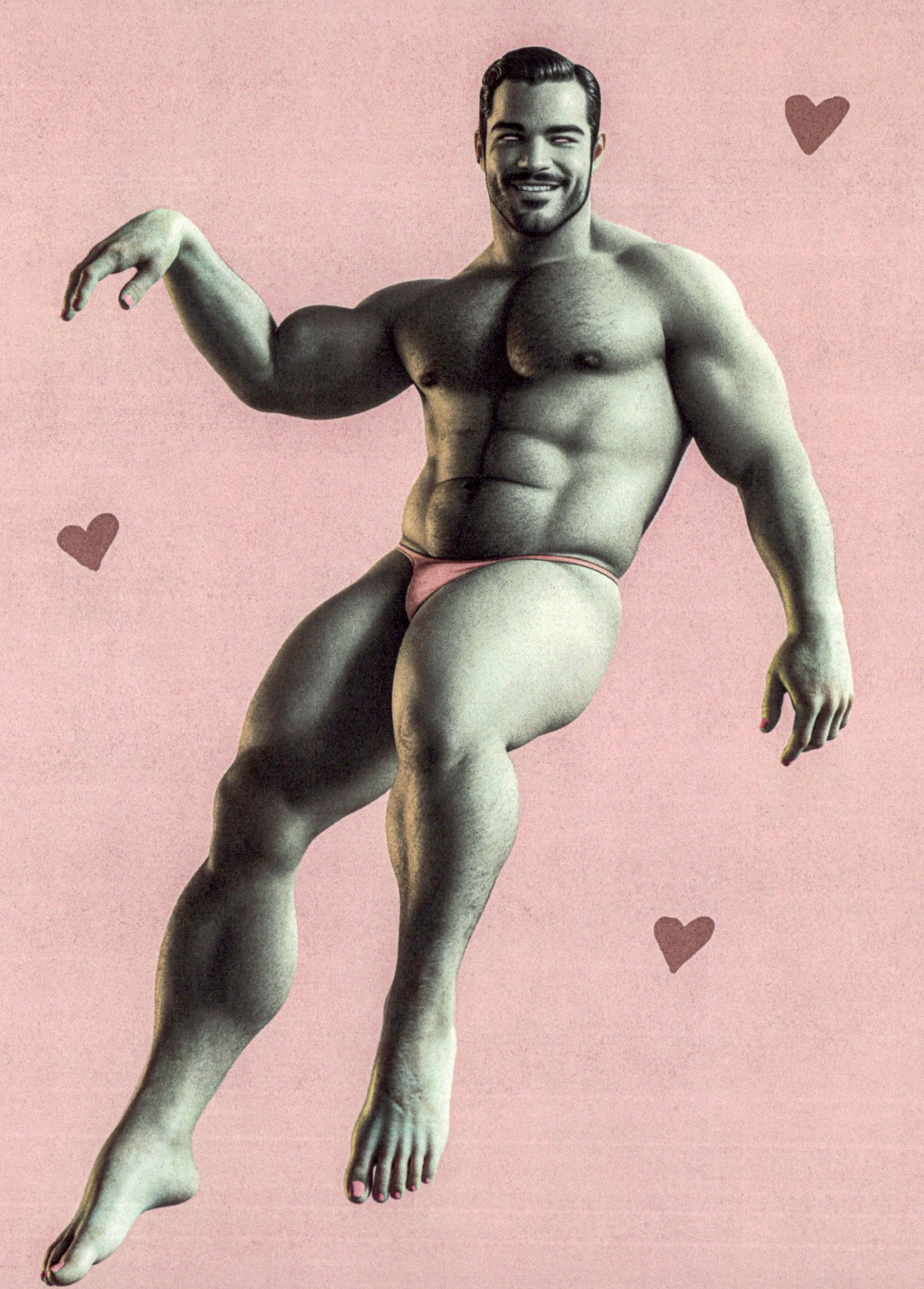

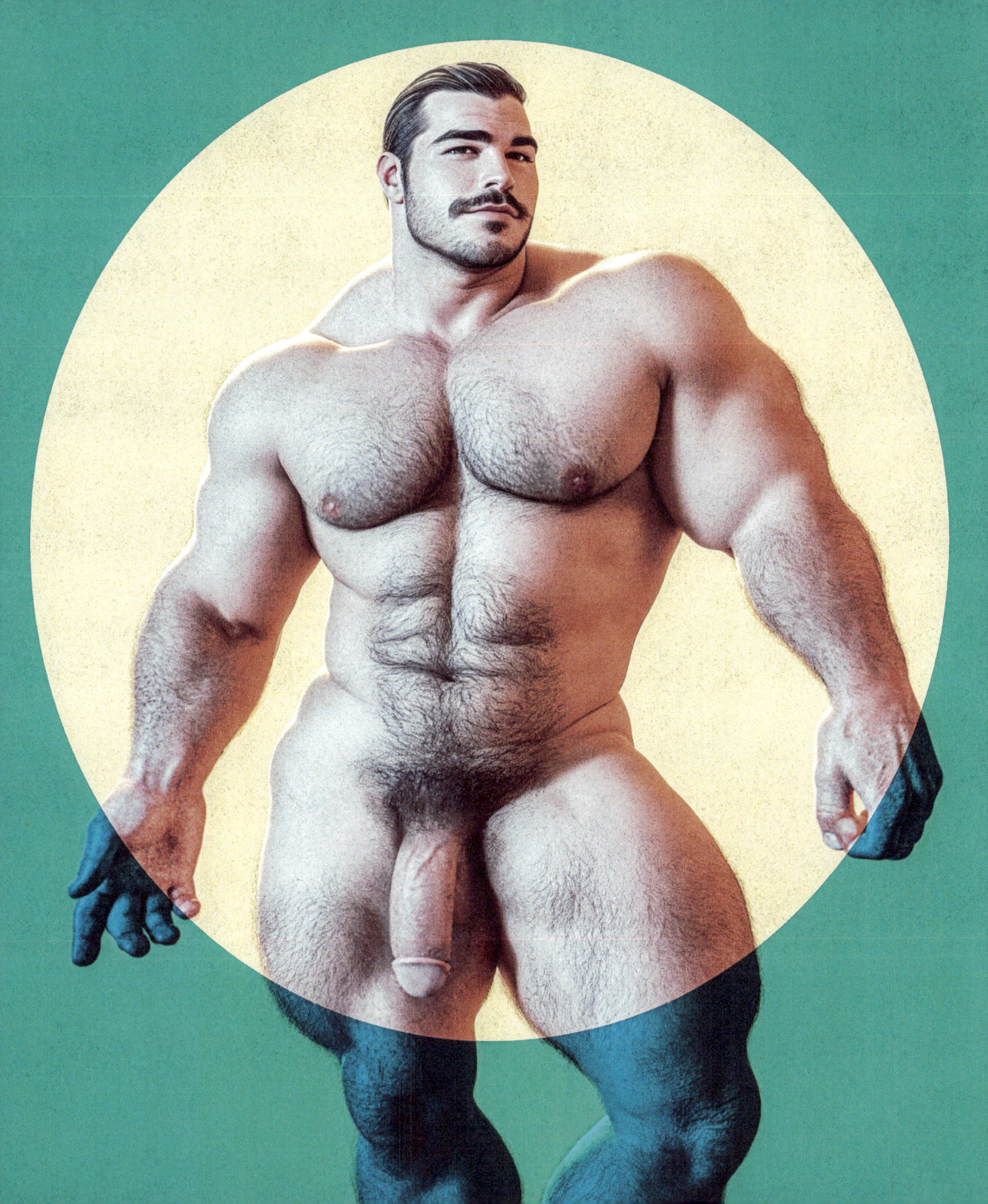

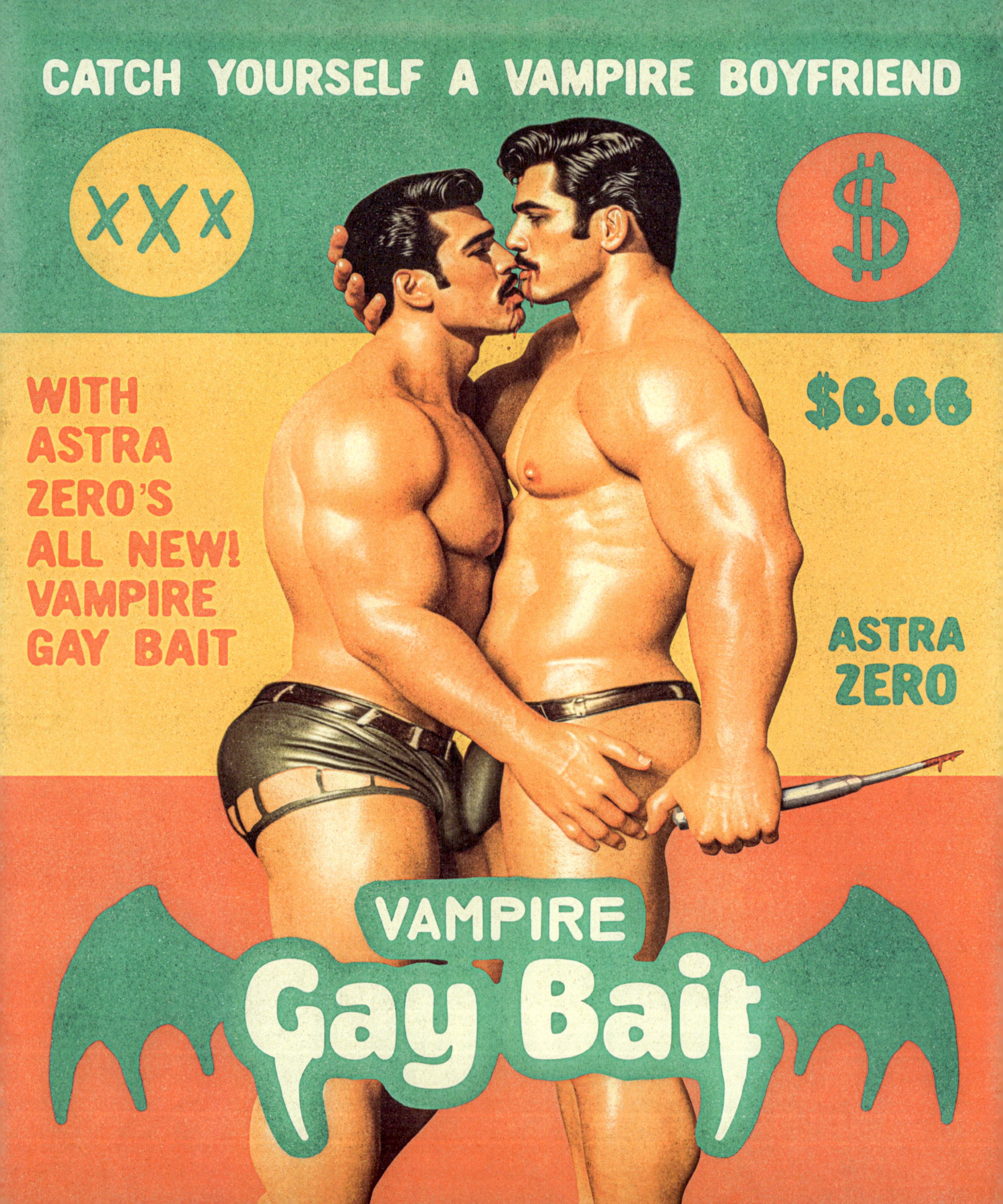

CATCH YOURSELF A VAMPIRE BOYFRIEND
XXX
$
WITH
ASTRA
ZERO'S
ALL NEW!
VAMPIRE
GAY BAIT
$6.66
ASTRA
ZERO
VAMPIRE
Gay Bait

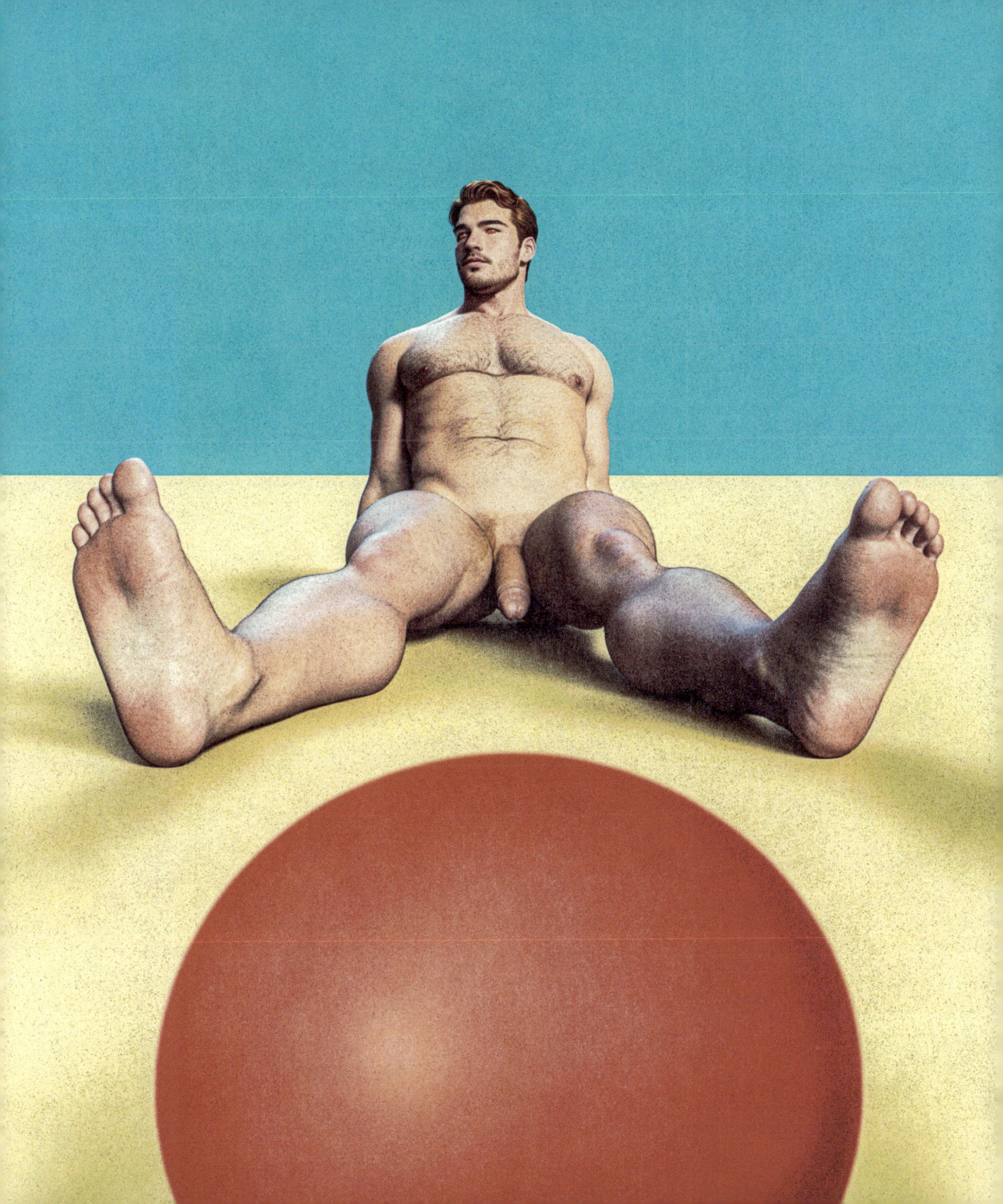

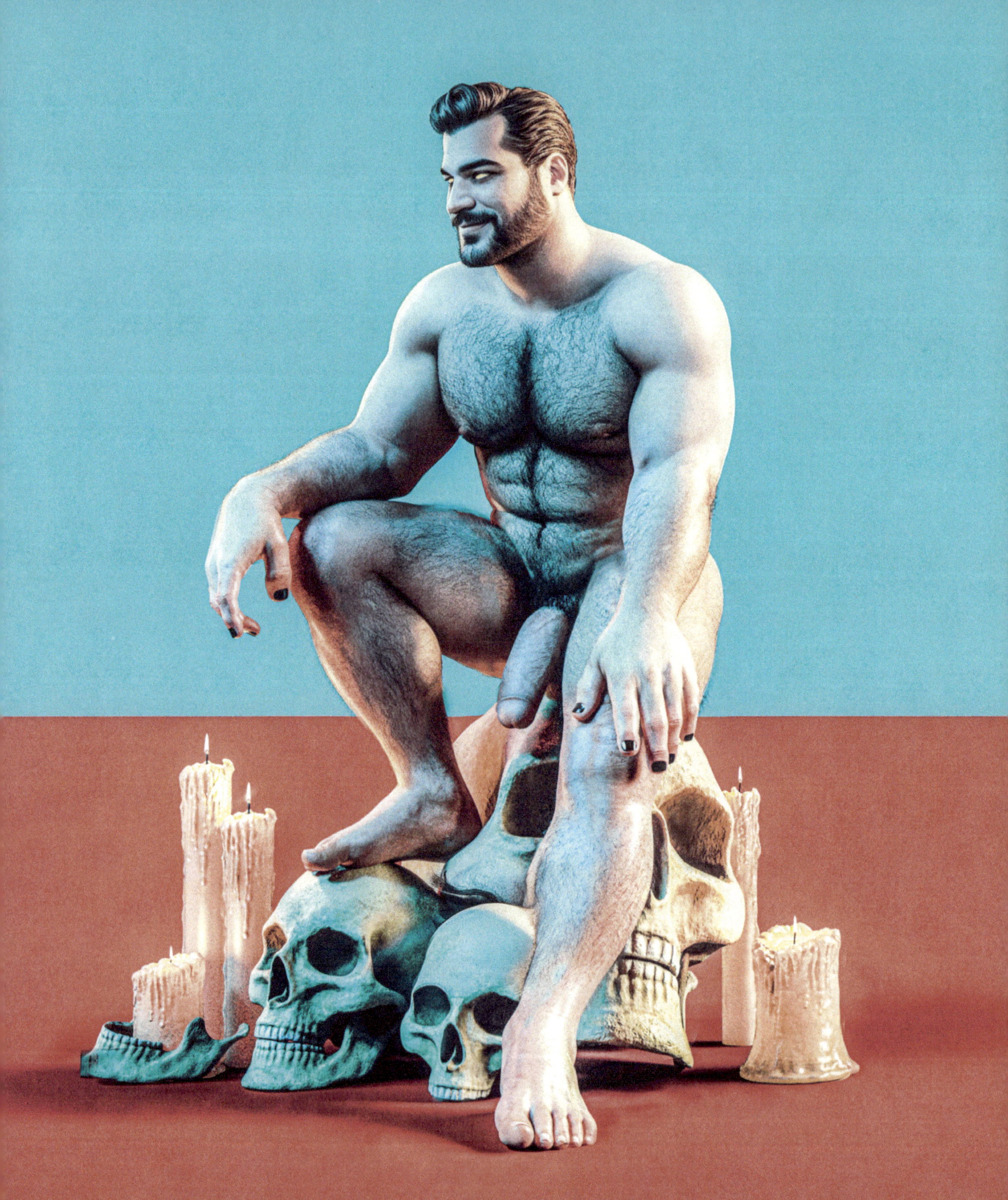

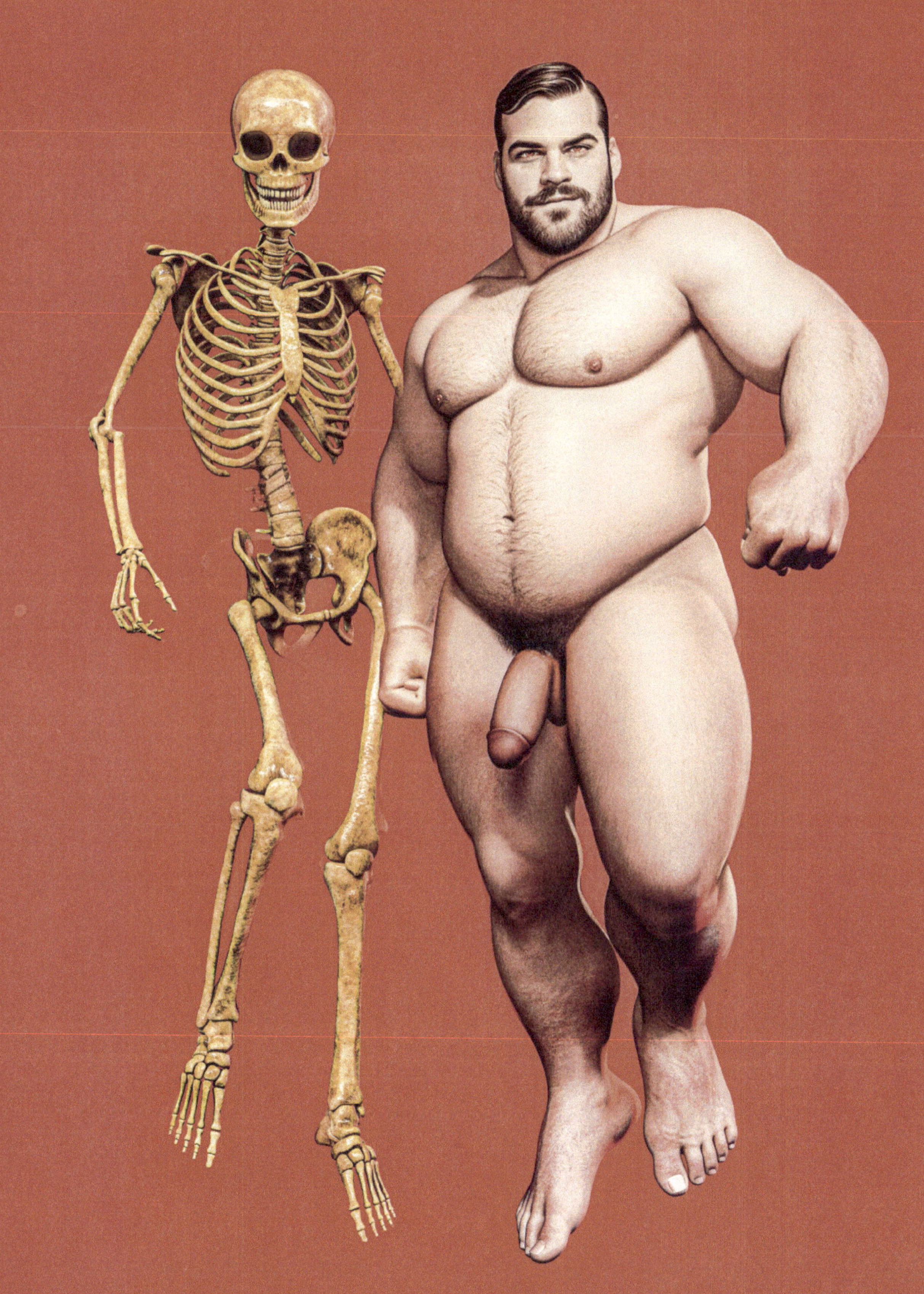

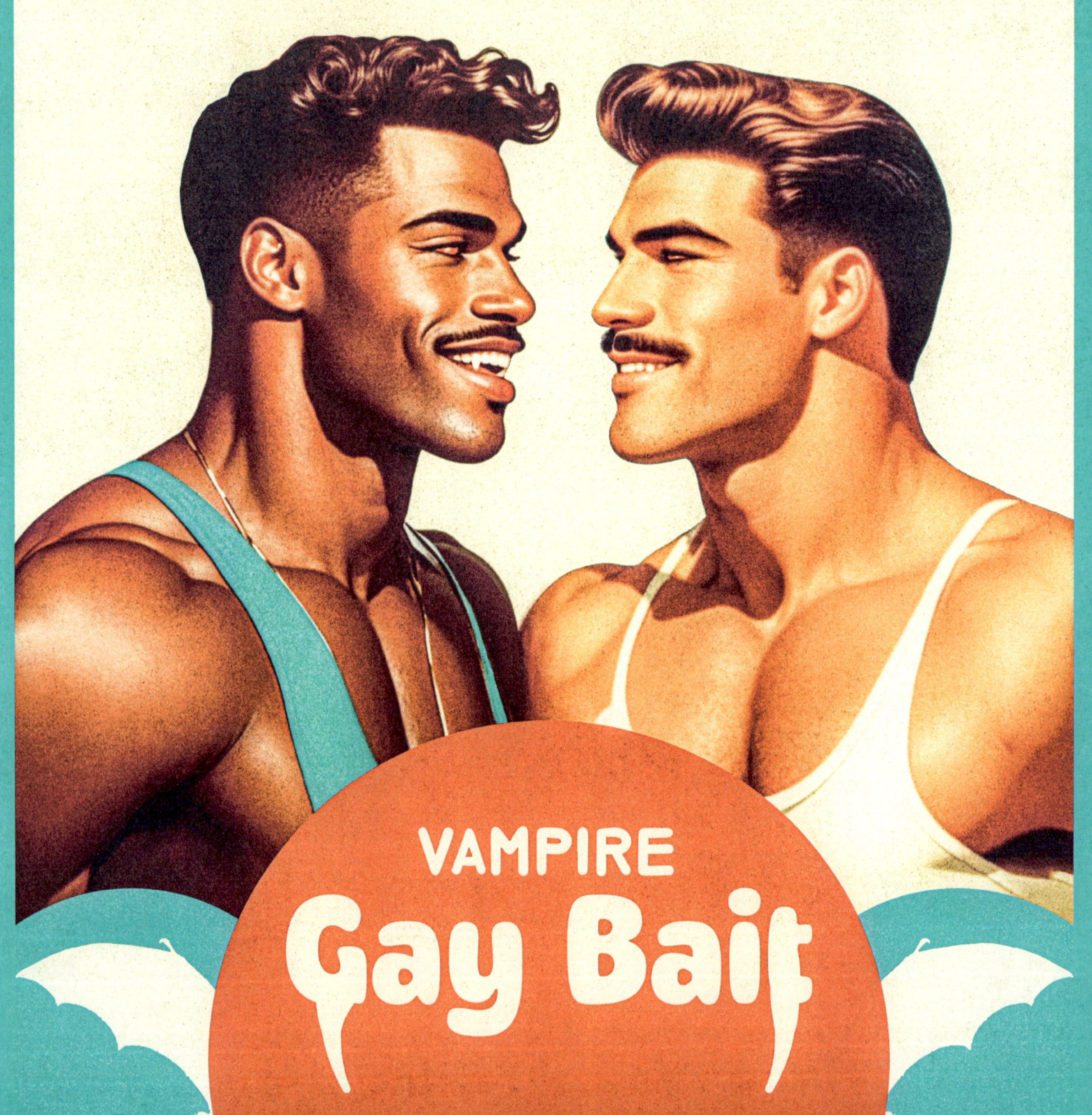

Catch yourself a Vampire Boyfriend!
With Astra Zero's all New Vampire Gay Bait
VAMPIRE
Gay Bait

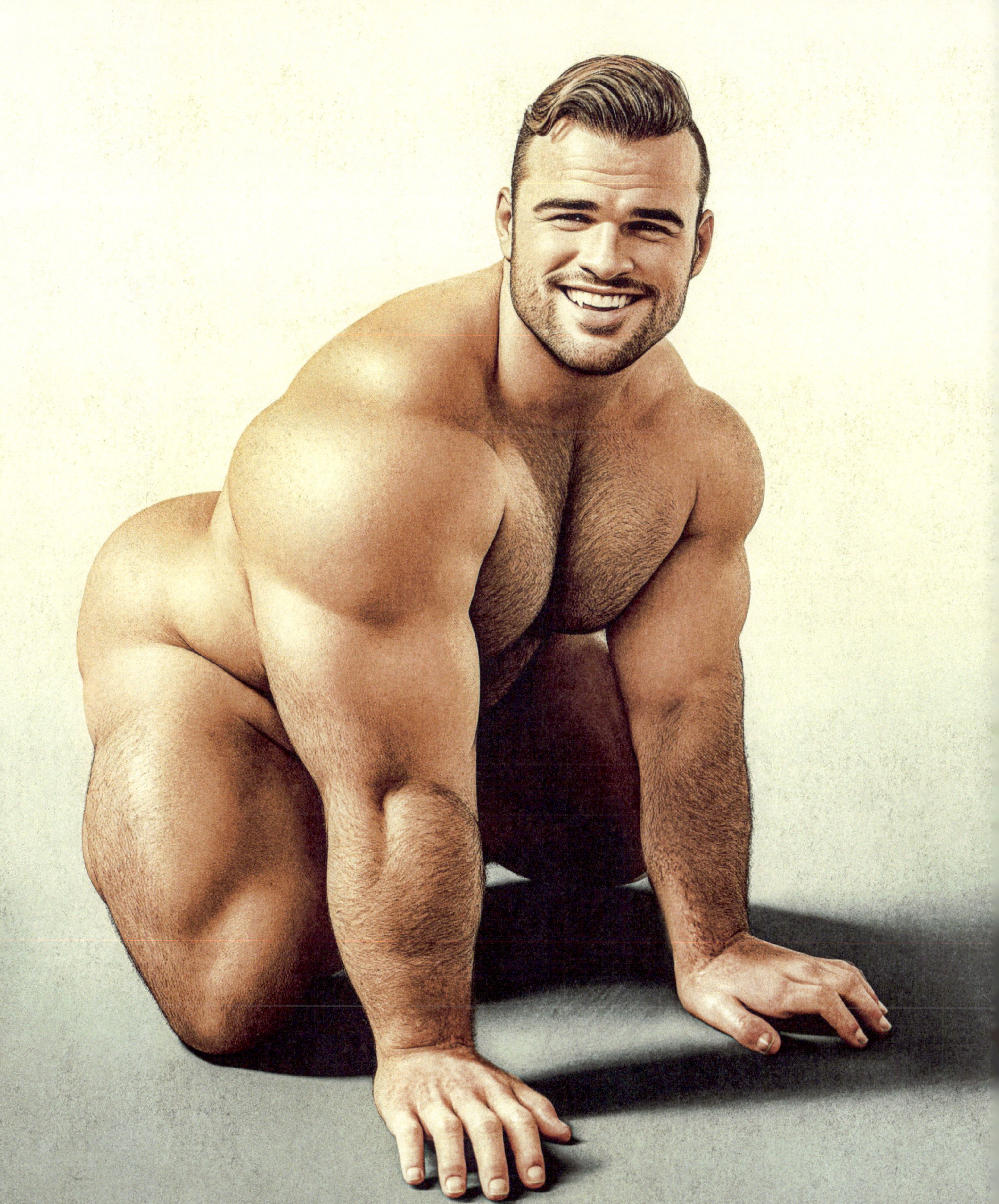

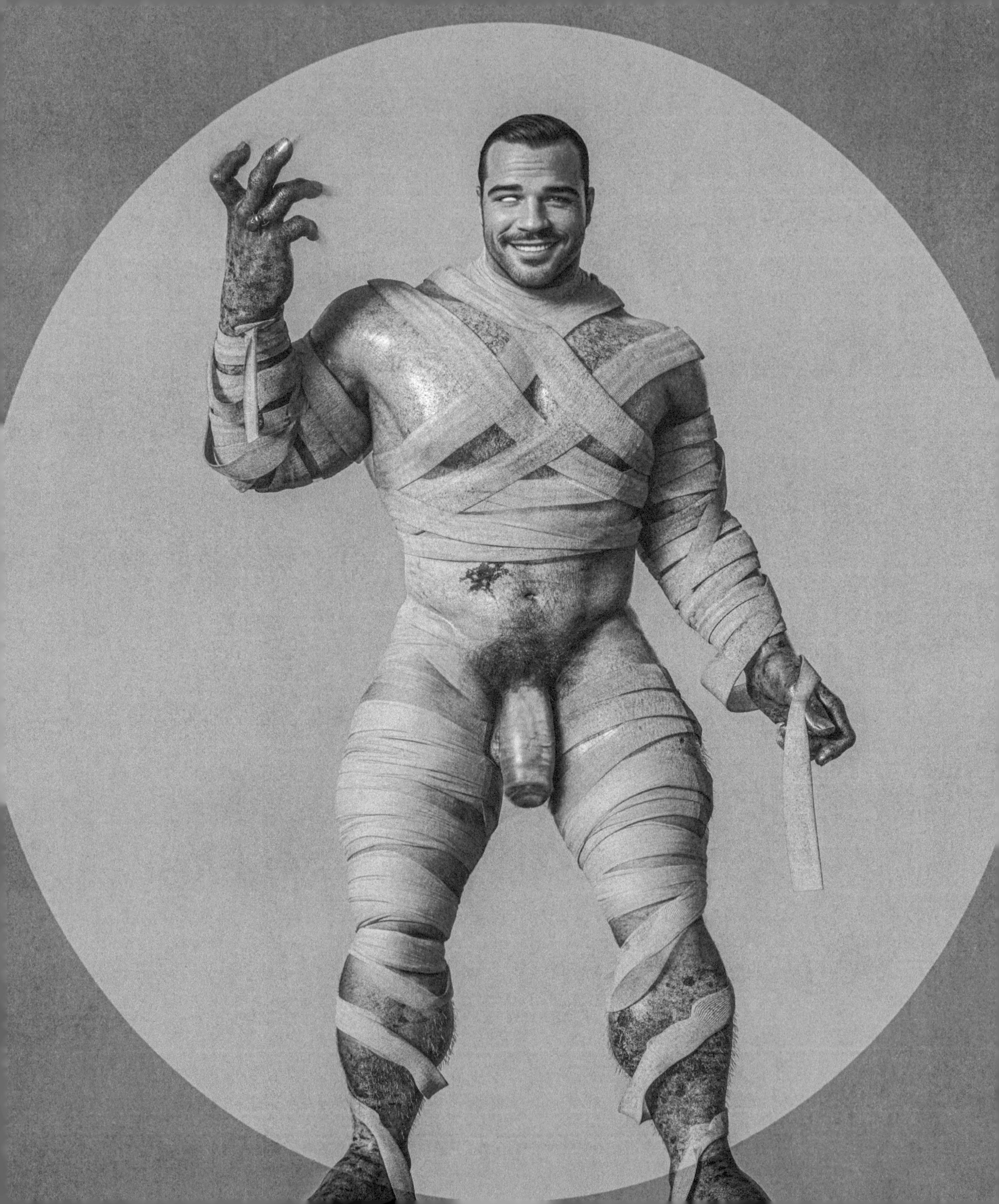

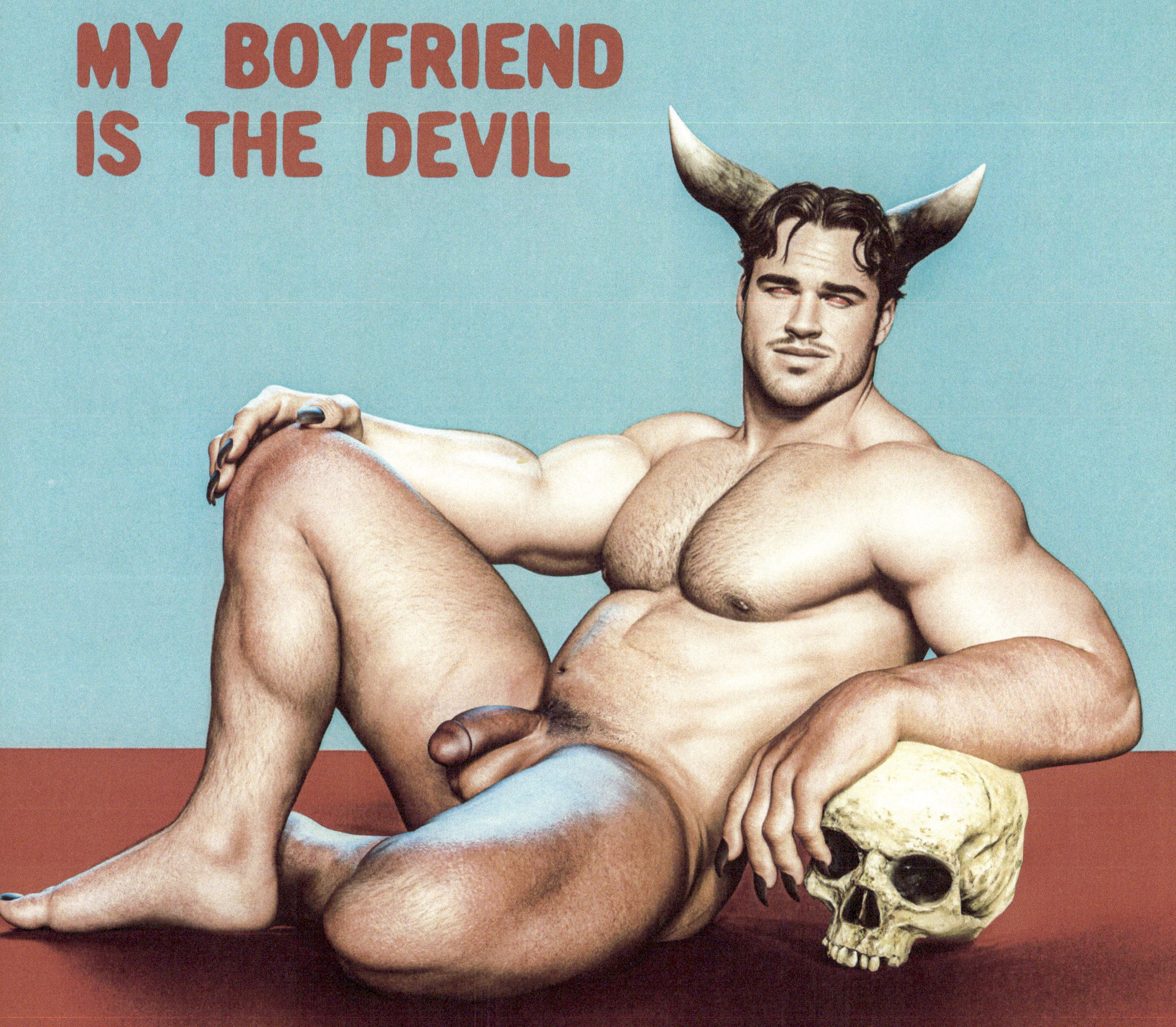

MY BOYFRIEND
IS THE DEVIL
BUT HE'S GREAT IN BED

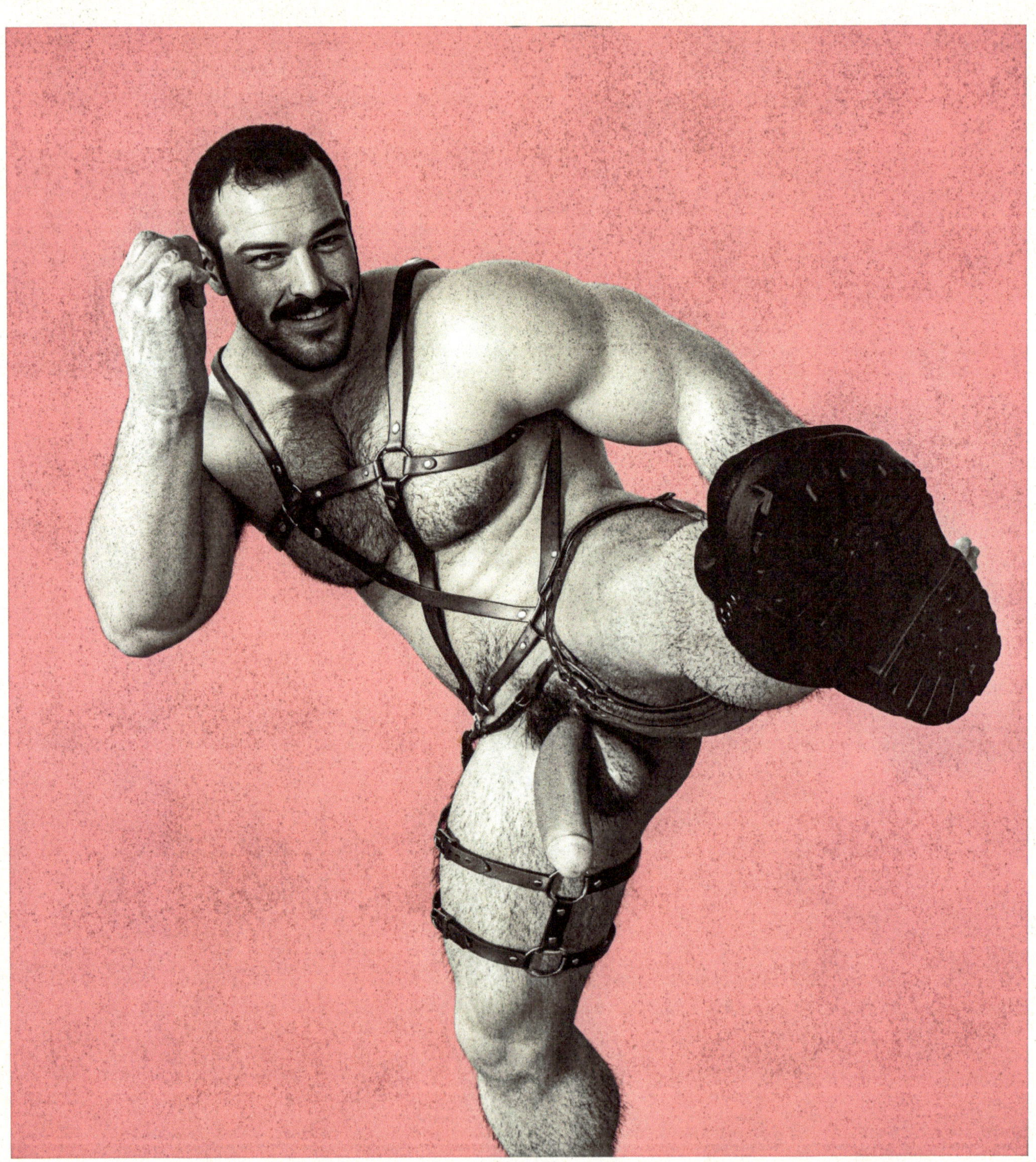

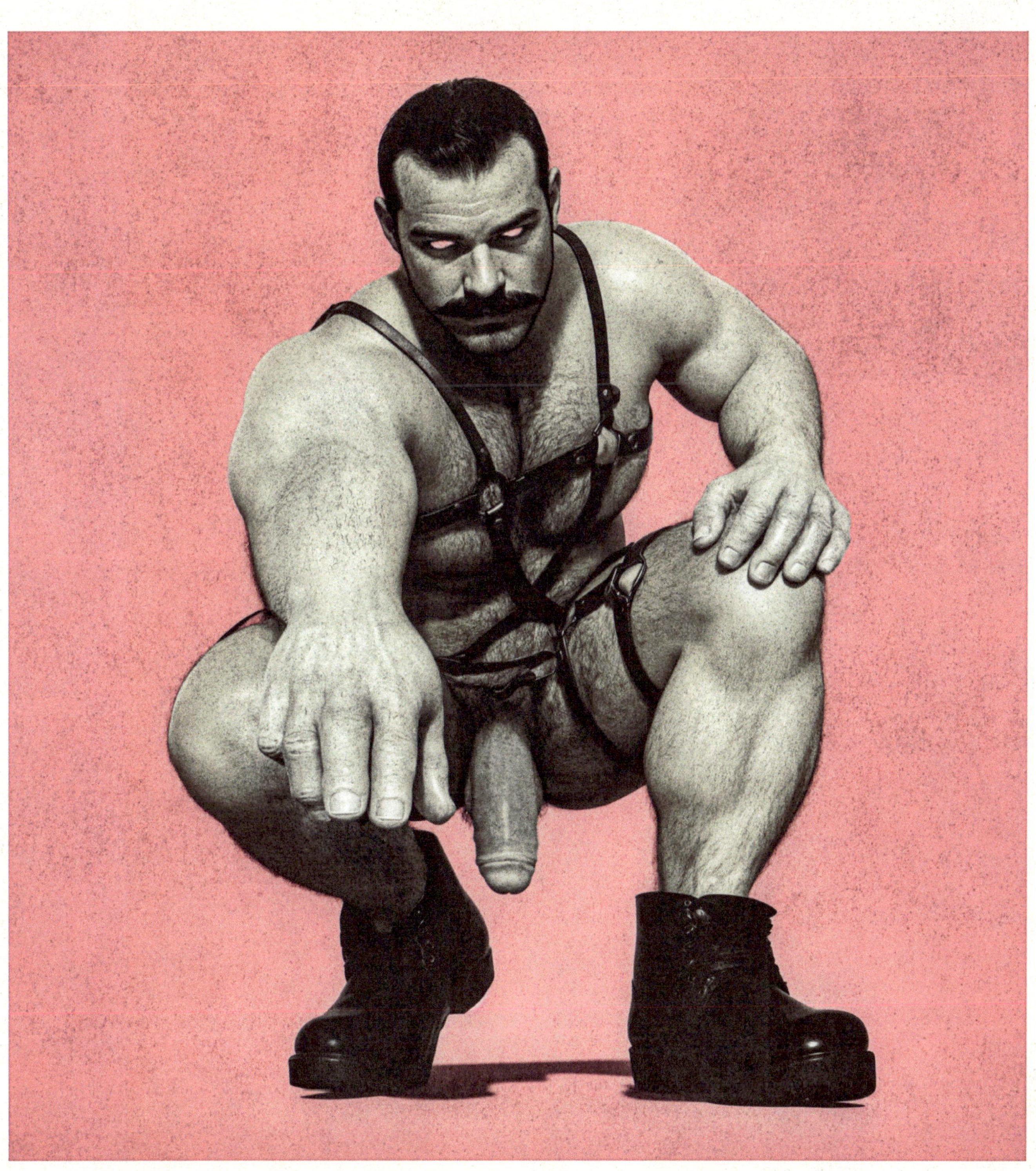

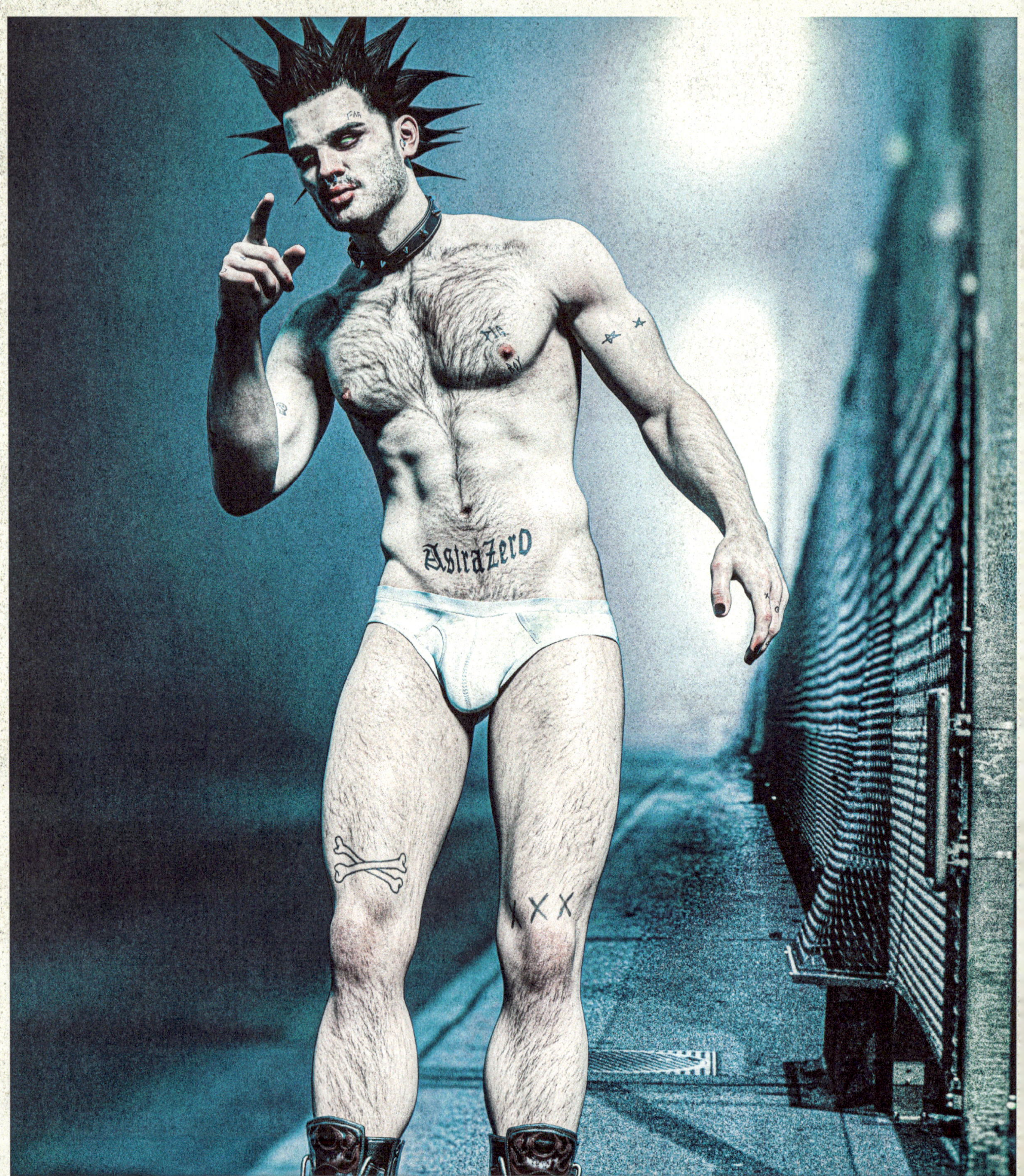
AstraZerO

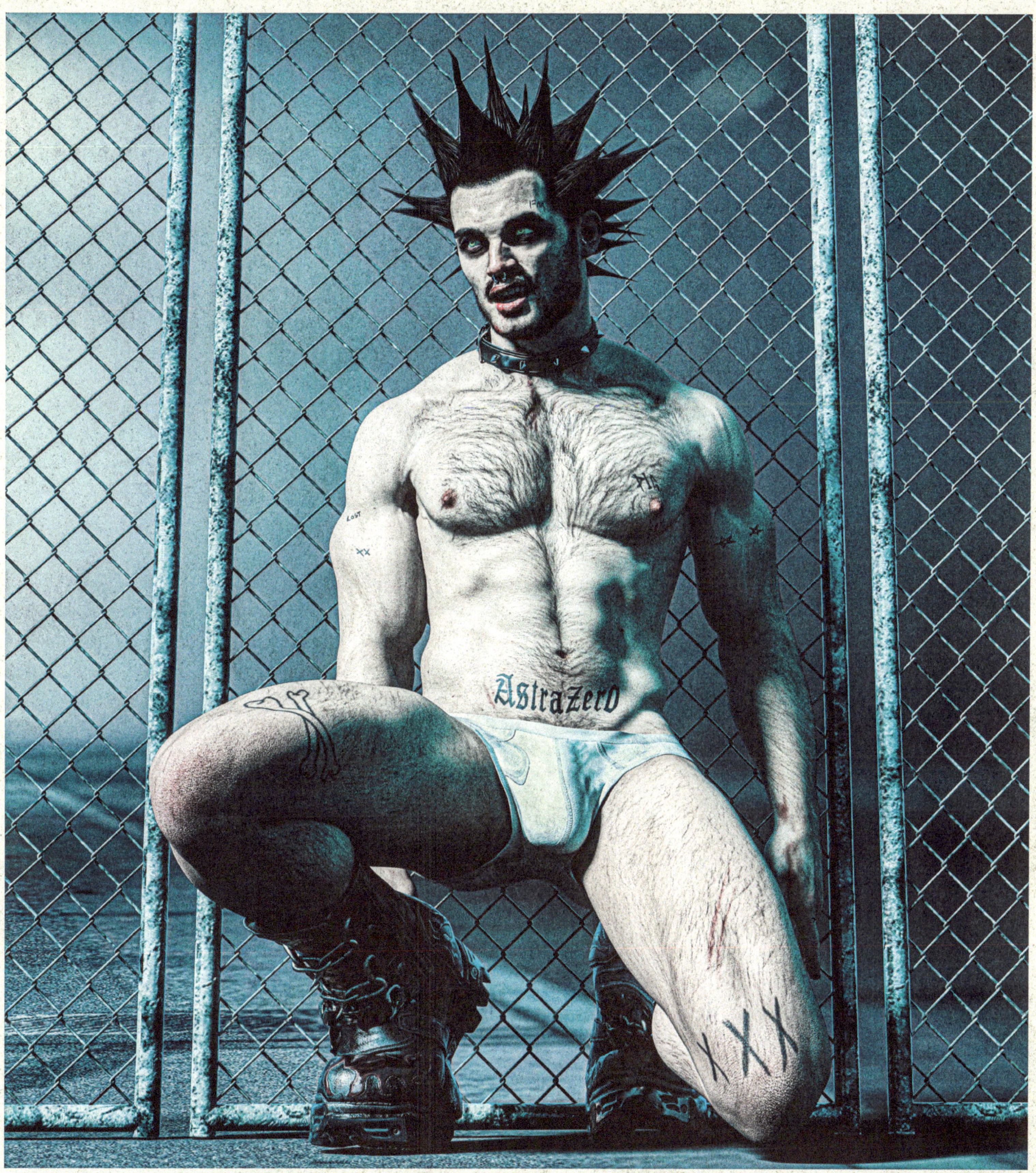

AstraZero
XXX

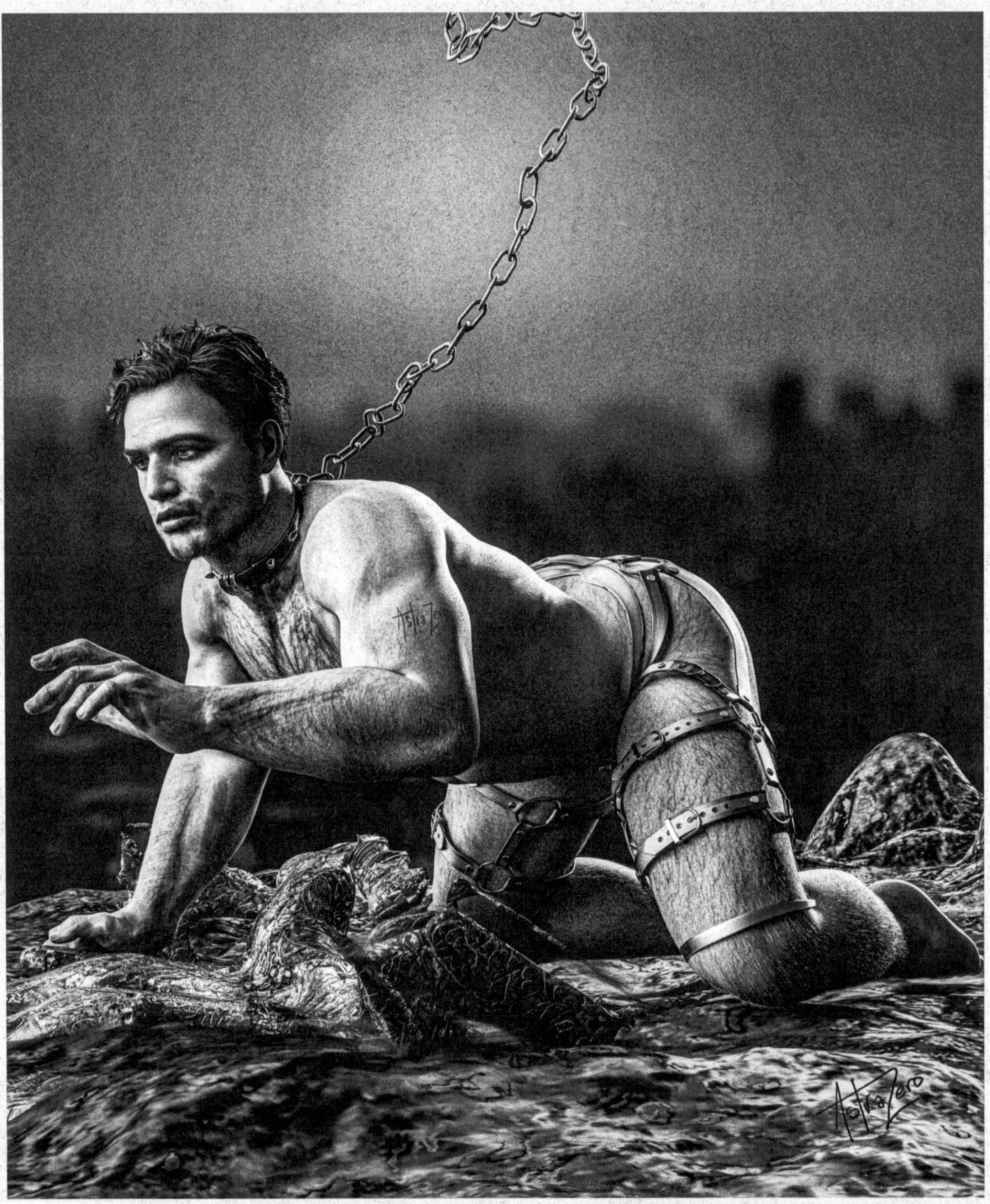

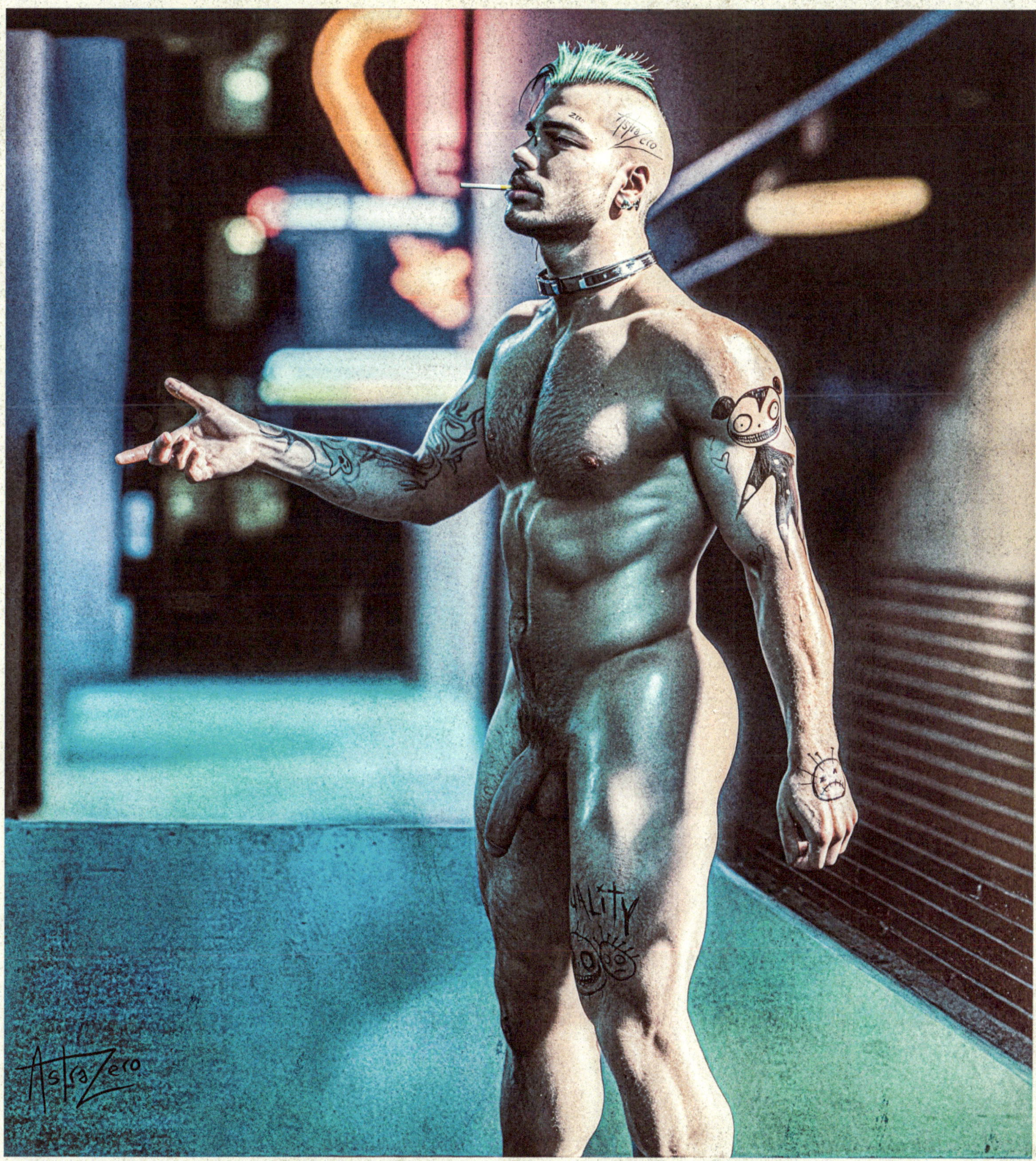

AstraZero

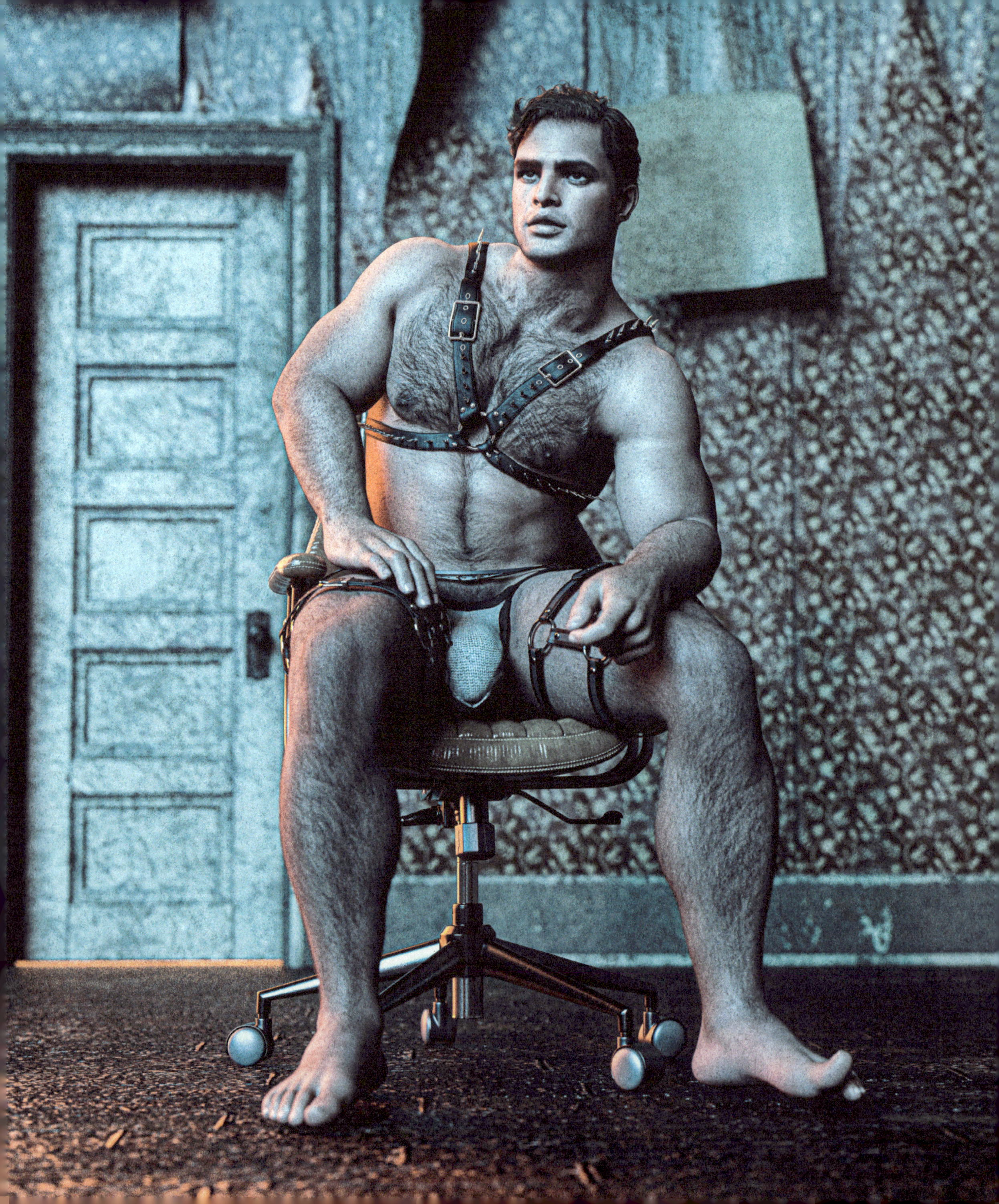

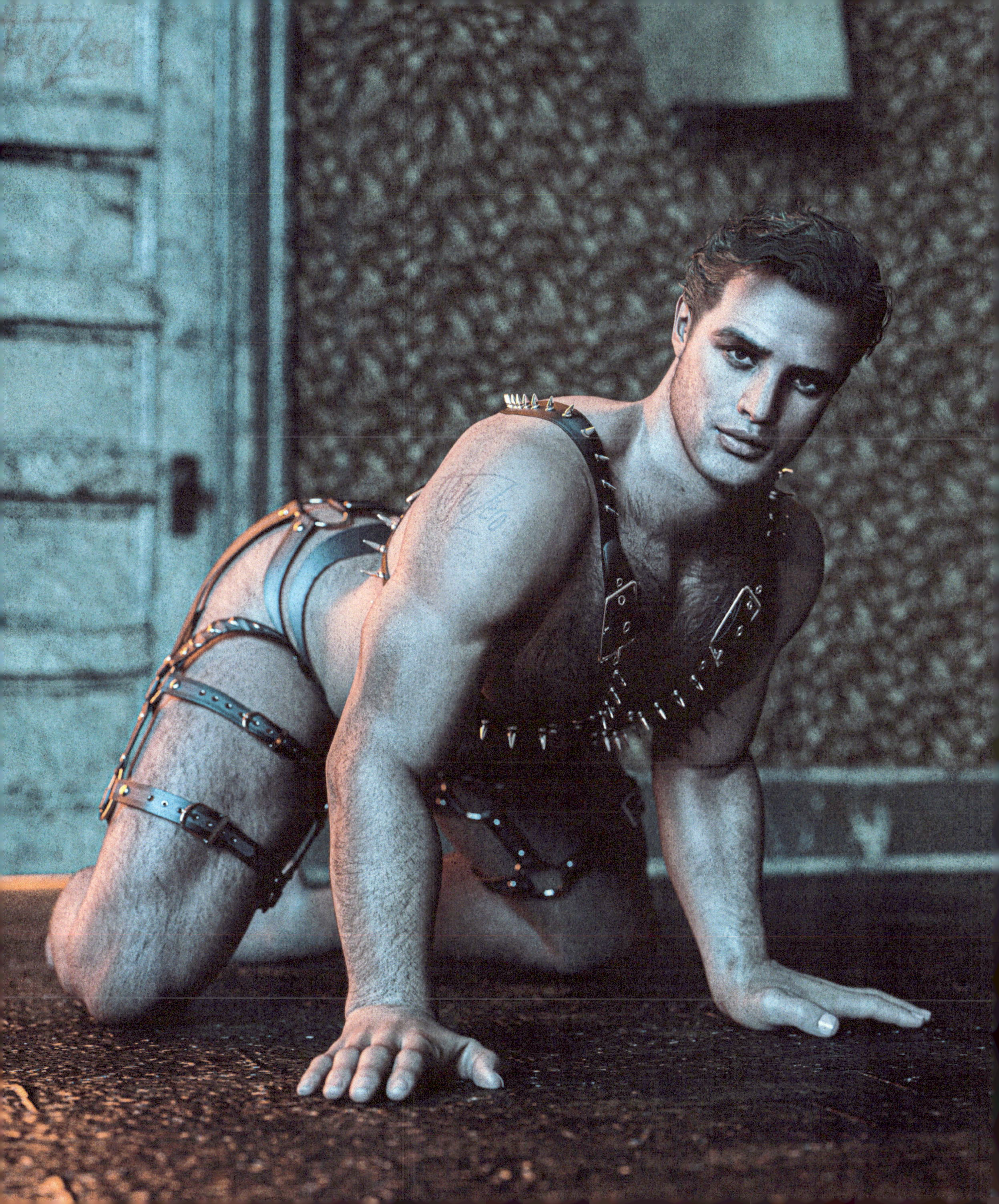

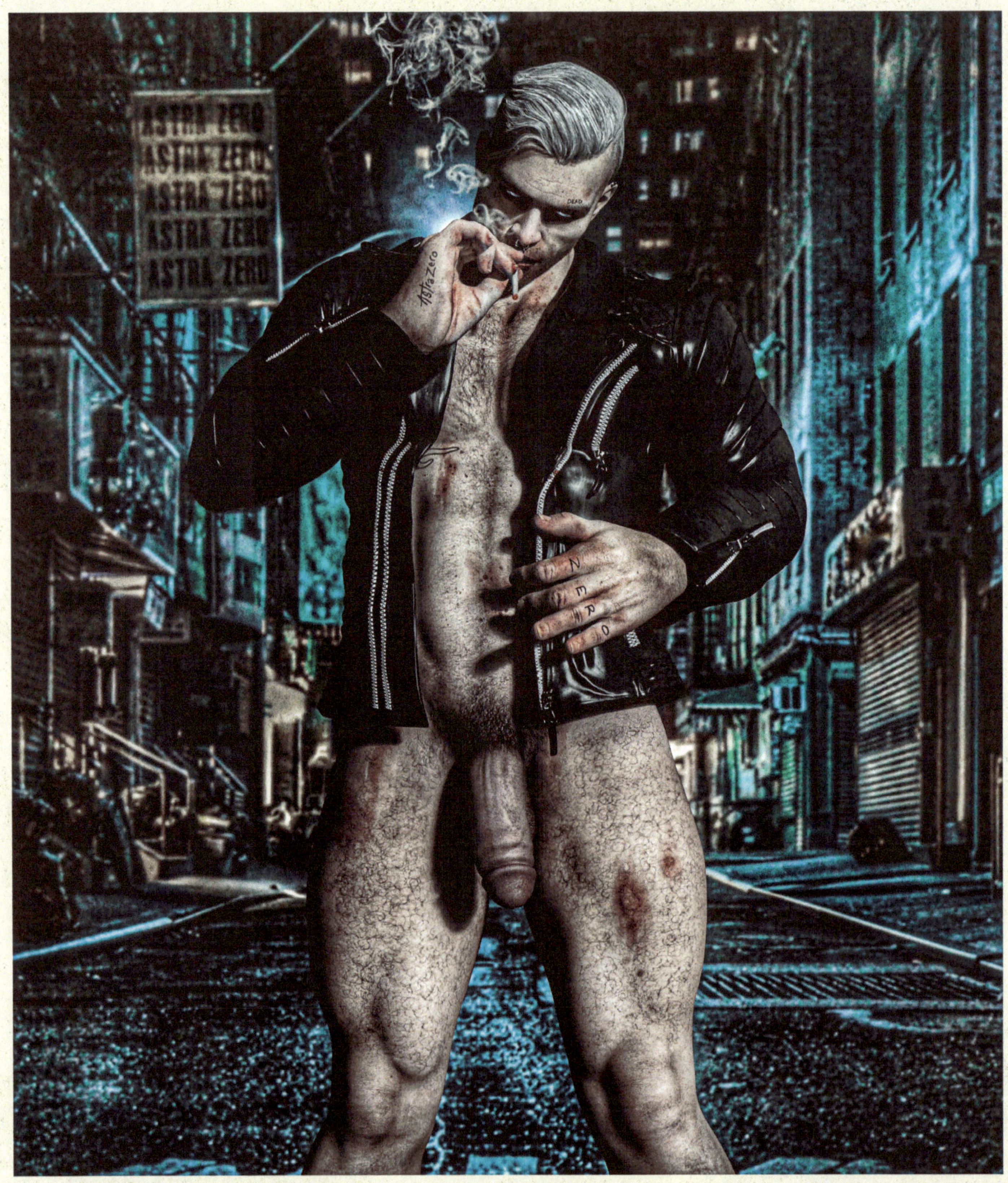
ASTRA ZERO
ASTRA ZERO
ASTRA ZERO
ASTRA ZERO
ASTRA ZERO

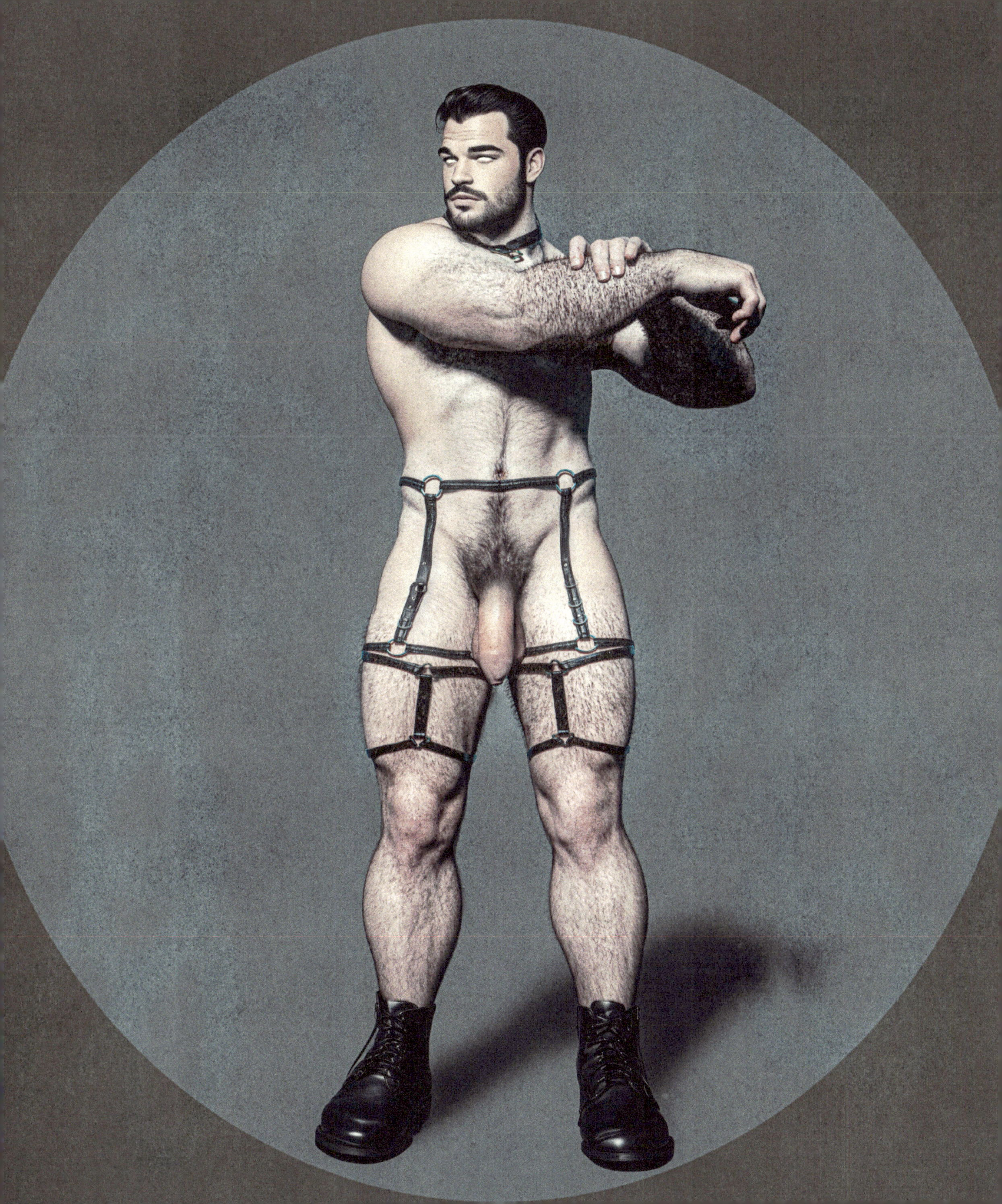

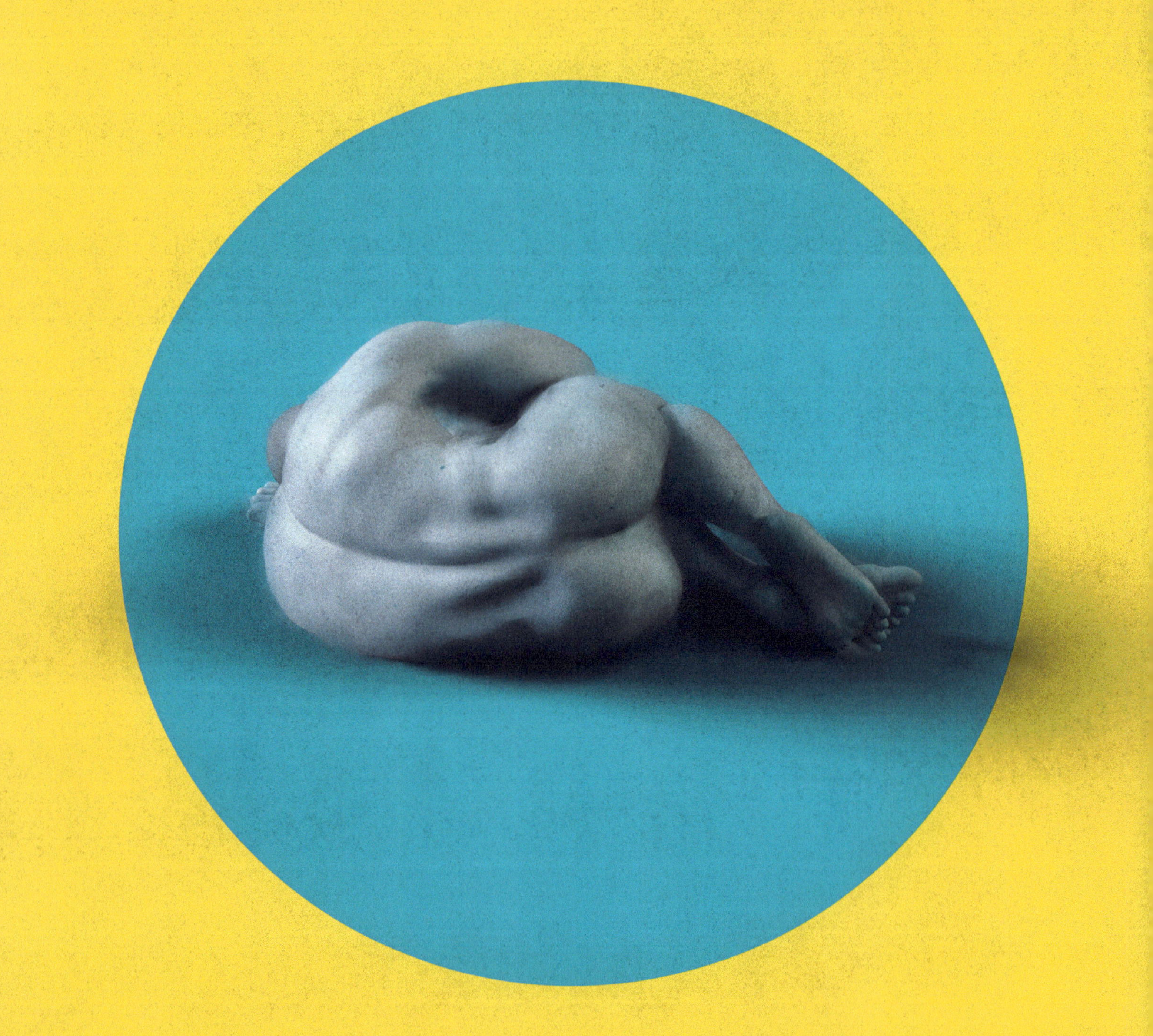

ABOUT THE ARTIST

Astra Zero (born Dustin Nicholls) is a queer Canadian alternative visual artist, designer, illustrator, video editor, creative director and songwriter.

His work fluctuates from a gothic macabre style and spooky cute themed visuals to his more popular sexually charged style of gay themed monsters, pop culture and historical revamped artwork with a dark erotic twist.

Starting off as a mainly 2D Artist with drawing & painting, His work has evolved to incorporate & mix more mediums and styles into his workflow, from Photography, 3D rendered work and digital painting, to animation, photo / video editing and graphic design.

You can see more of his work on social media @astrazero and on his website: www.astrazero.com

www.ingramcontent.com/pod-product-compliance
Lightning Source LLC
Chambersburg PA
CBHW042200030726
47599CB00004B/813